POETRY OF THE KOREAN WAR

POETRY OF THE KOREAN WAR

Edited by
Reuben Holroyd
The Duke of Wellington's Regiment

Published by
The British Korean Veterans Association

Copyright © poems retained by the authors.
Copyright © illustrations by Reuben Holroyd and Roger Phelps

All rights reserved. No reproduction, copy or transmission
of this publication, whether the whole or any part,
may be made without the prior written permission
of the editor and authors.

ISBN 0-9512622-1-1

First published 2003 by
The British Korean Veterans Association

Printed in Great Britain by
Reuben Holroyd Ltd
Hook House, Haley Hill, Halifax, West Yorkshire, HX3 6EE.

CONTENTS

Foreword		vii
Introduction		ix
OFF TO WAR		1
Departure	W. A. (Tony) Thorn	2
HMT Empire Orwell	John T. Boyd	3
I Was There	John T. Boyd	4
The Voyage Out	Douglas John Hollands	5
Off To War	Roy (Brummy) Reece	6
A Trip To War	Reg Briggs	7
Hell's Holiday Camp	A. R. (Tony) Sorrell & Friends	9
The Boys In Blue	Ken Gordon	10
THE LAND OF THE MORNING CALM		11
The Land Of The Morning Calm	Den Johnson	12
Korea	Ian E. Kaye	12
Old Mother-In-Law's Breath	Tony Thorn	13
Minus Forty	John T. Boyd	14
The Rain	Ian E. Kaye	15
The Sky Over Korea	John T. Boyd	16
Dawn Vigil	Anon	17
Then And Forever	Terry Moore	17
THE PITY OF WAR		19
Flotsam On The Tide	Ian E. Kaye	20
Korean Dawn	Keith Thomson	21
Scars Of War	Fred Kenrick	22
The Old Man And His Cow	Denis J. Woods	23
Soldier To Soldier	Ian E. Kaye	26
IN THE LINE		27
The Morning Calm	Colin Fowles	28
The Morning Calm	Peter Fisher	29
I Have	Ian E. Kaye	30
Yong Dong	Ken Cornwell	31
To A Patrol On 355	Ken Cornwell	31
Korean Incident	Ian E. Kaye	32
Aquila Non Capit Muscas	Ashley Cunningham-Boothe	32
Keep It Quiet	Ken Cornwell	33
A Letter Home	Robbie Lancaster	34
Got Your Mail	Reg Briggs	35
Wireless Operator	Kilroy of Nottingham	36
The Radio Operator	Reg Briggs	37
The Sniper	Douglas John Hollands	38
A Lost Friend	Douglas John Hollands	39
Song Of A Bird	Ian E. Kaye	39
A Worthless Hill	Roy Carswell	40
I'll Come To No Harm	Reg Briggs	41
The Barley Mow	William Gibson	42
The Korean Encounter	Bert Hutchings	43

Commission In Korea	Fred Kenrick	45
The Hook	D. Miller	46
The Saga Of The Comus	Buck Taylor	48
End Of The Journey	Ian E. Kaye	49
On Hearing News Of The Armistice	Ken Cornwell	50
IRREVERENT		51
Posted To The PBI	Douglas John Hollands	52
Follow The Leader	Ken Cornwell	54
Not Me Sir!	John T. Boyd	55
Advice To An Officer	Douglas John Hollands	56
A Squaddie's Lament	Alan Guy	56
Hell	Anon	57
Moving On	Anon	58
The General's Tool	Douglas John Hollands	60
CAPTIVITY		61
POW Camp 3, Korea 1952	D. S. Anderson	62
Thoughts	Anon	63
Prisoner Of War	Anon	64
A Photo & The Answer	Anon	65
When I Return	Anon	66
The Infantryman	Anon	67
Tender Lips & Hills Of Korea	Anon	68
REMINISCENCE		69
Our Pals	John T. Boyd	70
Bleak Day	Peter Fisher	71
At Rest	Anon	72
Ode To A Dead Cockney	Mike Mogridge	73
The Forgotten War	S. G. Buss	74
I Remember	Ron Leader	75
For Those Who Were There	Brian L. Porter	76
The Sixteen Hundred	Jack Arnall	77
Before Endeavours Fade	Denis J. Woods	78
Not Forgotten	T. J. Adkins	78
The Phantom Piper	W. A. (Tony) Thorn	79
Remembrance Day Reflections	Jim Jacobs	80
Korea	Roy (Brummy) Reece	81
Field Of Crosses	Denis Woods	82
United They Stood & The Korean Veteran	Alan Guy	83
Absent Veterans & The Memorial Bench	David Lidstone	84
British Soldier & Wars Will Never End	George E. Loudoun	85
The Sunday Parade	Bob Guess	86
Korean Veterans	Fred Almey	87
A Change Of Heart	Peter Fisher	88
Counselling	W. A. (Tony) Thorn	90
In Remembrance	W. A. (Tony) Thorn	93
Where Are You Now	Denis J. Woods	94
50th Anniversary	R. Miller	96

FOREWORD

Towards the end of World War II the United Soviet Socialist Republic (USSR) occupied Korea, a former Japanese colony, and advanced down the peninsula to be met by troops of the United States of America moving northwards. They met at the 38th Parallel and agreement was reached to divide the country at this point into the Democratic People's Republic of Korea (DPRK) in the North and the Republic of Korea (ROK) in the South.

This division remained in place until 25th June 1950 when units of the North Korean People's Army (NKPA), led by Russian built T-34 tanks, crossed the 38th Parallel and invaded the ROK. The post World War II Cold War was now hotting up.

The ROK appealed to the United Nations Security Council for assistance. A Council Resolution called for the immediate cessation of hostilities, the withdrawal of North Korean communist troops to the 38th Parallel and for all members of the United Nations to help in restoring peace.

Sixteen countries responded by supplying combat forces, namely: the United States of America, Great Britain, Canada, Australia, New Zealand, South Africa, Netherlands, Belgium (incorporating a platoon from Luxembourg), France, Turkey, Greece, Ethiopia, Thailand, Colombia and the Philippines. Plus of course the armed forces of the Republic of Korea.

Non-combatant support was contributed by units from: Sweden, Norway, Denmark, India and Italy who was not a member of the United Nations.

The Royal Navy was the first into action. With twenty-two ships in the Far East in June 1950, and several in Japanese waters, it was able to give immediate help.

The Fleet consisted of two headquarters ships, six cruisers, seven destroyers, fourteen frigates, seventeen Royal Fleet auxiliary vessels, and one hospital ship.

Four aircraft carriers patrolled the west coast. Eleven squadrons of aircraft flew from the carriers throughout the war. Consisting of one squadron of Seafires, five of Sea Furies and five of Fireflies.

The Royal Marines included 41 Independent Commando.

The Army sent two infantry battalions from the Hong Kong garrison. Followed by another fourteen infantry battalions, four tank regiments, four artillery regiments and many other supporting units from Britain. A large fleet of troopships sailed back and forth between Britain and Korea, taking out reinforcements and bringing home time expired men.

The Royal Air Force had two squadrons of Sunderland flying boats stationed at Iwakuni, Japan. Two RAF Flights 1903 and 1913 of light observation aircraft were attached to the Commonwealth Division. RAF pilots flew fighter planes through attachment to the Australian 77 Fighter Squadron and the American 16 Fighter Interception Squadron of 51 Fighter Interception Wing. The planes were British Meteor jets and American F86 Sabre jets.

The climate of Korea runs to extremes, from bitterly cold winters to hot, humid summers. The terrain was harsh and unforgiving, especially for infantry personnel. Destruction by advancing and retreating armies was commonplace. Scenes of utter devastation of cities, towns and villages was the norm. Death and carnage pervaded the whole country.

The first twelve months was that of a mobile war as armies moved up and down the peninsula. But by the summer of 1951 the war had become a static one. With a fortified trench system, roughly along the 38th Parallel, reminiscent of the First World War fought in Europe. But with one big difference. In both World Wars when troops were out of the line they returned to the comfort of a normal barracks routine, and within reach of the amenities of civilization. Not so in Korea. A tented rest camp out of the range of enemy guns, set among barren hills and disused paddyfields, was home behind the line. Entertainment was an open air film show, while an occasional visit by a concert party was a major event.

Once settled in most battalions never moved from their brigade area during the twelve months or more of service in Korea. In that period each soldier was allowed one week's leave in Tokyo, and five days' leave at Inchon Rest Centre on the coast.

The total casualties have never been accurately determined. The largest losses were suffered by the Republic of Korea and the United States. United Nations' casualties amounted to more than 14,000 of which the British share was 1,078 dead, 2,674 wounded and 1,060 missing or prisoners. Additionally 53 Britons died while serving in the Australian Army and are included in the Australian casualty figures.

Enemy casualties are harder to quantify. Neither the Chinese or North Koreans ever admitted their losses. The Allied Joint Chiefs of Staff's summary of 27th July 1953 gives the following estimates. Chinese: 401,401 killed. 486,995 wounded and 21,211 captured. North Koreans: 214,899 killed, 303,685 wounded, and 101,680 missing or captured. It was calculated that between two and a half and three million Korean civilians perished in the war.

The fighting ceased on 27th July 1953, but British troops continued to serve on the Kansas Line for a further four years, the last combat troops leaving Korea in July 1957.

There was no victory, and still today soldiers of the ROK Army and the United States 2nd Indian Head Division still guard the 38th Parallel, a few of them grandchildren of the men who fought there fifty years ago.

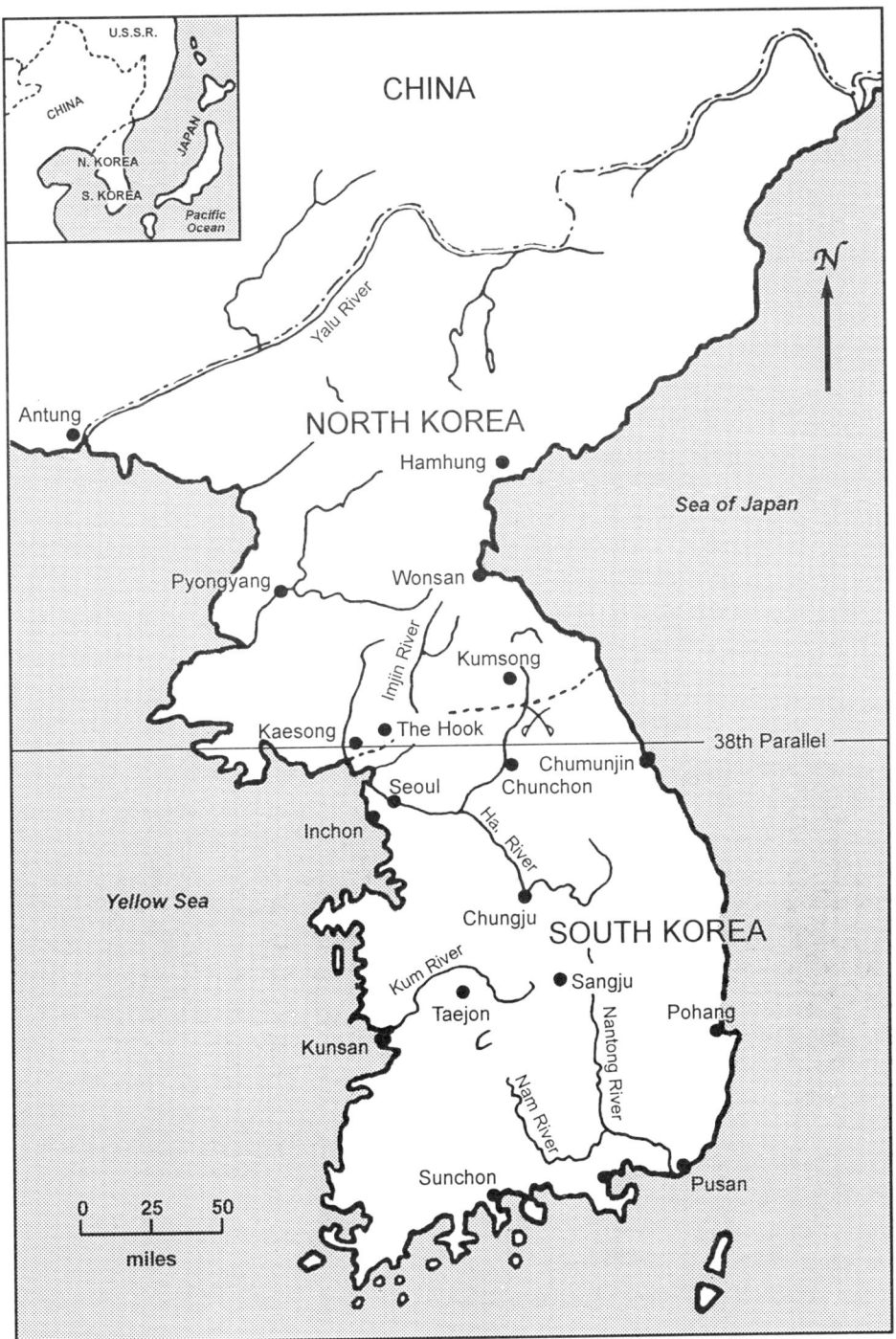

This book is dedicated to the memory of all who lost their lives while serving in British and other Commonwealth forces in the Korean War.

"Not One of Them is Forgotten before God"

OFF TO WAR

DEPARTURE

In June 1952 I boarded the troopship Devonshire in Liverpool with the rest of my battalion, 1 King's Regiment, bound for Hong Kong and then Korea.

Two years later I was on my way home again, this time aboard the troopship Empire Halladale. But instead of being a fit young subaltern who had proudly carried the Colours on our departure, I now lay paralysed in the ship's hospital, having suffered a near-fatal attack of polio. But then I was the lucky one. My fellow subaltern, who carried the Regimental Colour on that same occasion, was killed while on patrol in December 1952 and he now lies with the others in the United Nations' Cemetery in Pusan.

Come all you lads from Liverpool,
The troopship's in the bay,
The tide is on the turn at last,
It's time you sailed away.

You've taken leave of Mum and Dad,
And Bessie down the road.
And proudly marched down Castle Street,
So full, it overflowed.

The band is playing 'Auld Lang Syne',
The tears are falling fast.
As flies the regimental flag,
So nobly from the mast.

The sound of sirens fill the air,
From ships on either side.
As seawards, ever faster now,
You sail upon the tide.

Just one last look before we go,
One wave and then it's done.
"Take care, 'Godspeed', just watch yourself,
And come back safe my son!"

W. A. (Tony) Thorn
1 King's Regiment (Liverpool)

H.M.T. EMPIRE ORWELL

Here we sail in swinging billets on our way to far-off lands.
We watch the dolphins swim before us
and hear the tunes of marching bands.
On a great white floating barracks
painted round with royal blues,
dressed olive greens and khaki drill, one thousand pairs of plimsoll shoes.

From Southampton's muddy waters, down the English Channel to
the Bay of Biscay (see that porpoise).
Past the coast of Spain and through
the Med, past Gib, and Malta's Cross;
then Port Said in view.
Sail the Cut and Bitter Lakes - Ismailiya - just passing through.

Heading south to Gulf of Suez; nothing there but sand and sand.
Red Sea takes us further southwards
to Aden's barren rocks so grand.
We cross the Indian Ocean's vastness -
furthest here from any land -
to Colombo's wide green city, look! there's a lighthouse in the strand.

Four hours stop and east - we round Sumatra to the Malay Straits.
Singapore we stop at next
where natives wear their hats like plates.
The tropic sun, it burns our knees
as we sail South China Seas,
to Kowloon Port, Hong Kong and what they call New Territories.

The Empire Orwell steams on north from the Cancer tropic heat,
through the Old Formosa straits
past two Chinas - where they meet -
to where Korea's rocks provide
a harbour and a shanty town.
'Busiest Military Port' - Pusan - where the infantry put down.

The troopship takes us further east to the Land of the Rising Sun,
where the islands rise to greet us
from the sea - our journey done.
Eight hours east, ten thousand miles
half a hemisphere away from
those other offshore islands, from our homes and yesterday.

John T. Boyd
Royal Signals, King Troop, 28 Brigade

I WAS THERE!

You ask me where I've been and I'll tell what I've seen
in my two years with the Colours in the line.
Five hundred thousand men were under arms just then
and several million more were marking time.
I can tell you what it meant, sleeping fourteen to a tent
and washing in a stream - 'cause I was there!

In the year of '51 we were called up one by one
to serve our Country, Empire and the King.
There were wars in several spots and some were really hot
and to get a foreign posting was the thing.
So I volunteered to go, as far as Tokyo;
to the far east and Korea - and I was there!

We sailed across the seas and the sun that burnt our knees
beat down upon the open desert sands.
The setting sun at night switched off - just like a light -
and we saw the moon and stars from many lands.
We mounted many guards and we didn't find it hard.
I remember it so well - for I was there!

On a cool and placid sea, with it's load of soldiery
the troopship rumbled on towards the dawn.
Across the ocean deep, to the gods that never sleep
in a country where the people were forlorn.
They were fighting hard for life against the tyranny of strife
and I joined them in that fight while I was there!

Those oriental maidens have hair as black as ravens
and their gentle eyes are deepest darkest brown.
They could capture any heart - although you soon would part,
for the army didn't stay long in one town.
I never will forget! - I'd even take a bet
that someone will remember I was there!

It's rather nice to roam, but now I've got back home
I think I'd like to stay and settle down.
My adventure's in the past. (I hope it's not my last!)
My knees are very definitely brown.
So now I'll swing the light with all my merry might
so you will all be certain - I was there!

John T. Boyd
Royal Signals, King Troop, 28 Brigade

THE VOYAGE OUT

For those who lack the will to wander
And whose spirit is pathetically inert,
The sight of the sea and all points yonder
Will perchance their outlook convert.
Away we go, my muckers, the whole wide world to see.
Many a sight we'll gawp at, but not for a tourist fee.

For many of our lads it was just such a case.
First, Gibraltar standing lonesome and mighty,
Then in the Med, dolphins leaping with grace,
And in Cyprus a meeting with Aphrodite.
Away we go, my muckers, the whole wide world to see.
Many a sight we'll gawp at, but not for a tourist fee.

Then down into Suez, the bowels of the earth,
With a dubious smell that smacked of hell
And bum boats swarming like flies as we berth,
Each piled to the gunnels with junk to sell.
Away we go, my muckers, the whole wide world to see.
Many a sight we'll gawp at, but not for a tourist fee.

We come to rest between Pusan's piers,
And when ashore our Colours are paraded.
The sound of our band dispels all fears
And hopes of victory are upgraded.
Away we go, my muckers, the whole wide world to see.
Many a sight we'll gawp at, but not for a tourist fee.

Douglas John Hollands
The Duke of Wellington's Regiment

OFF TO WAR

On board the troopship sailing to war
With bodies all sweating and vomit galore.
Where is Korea the young soldier said?
As he lay in his hammock that now was his bed.
Some say it's in China or is it Japan
Or is it in Russia perhaps it's Taiwan.

We have heard of this war in a far away place,
Where East fights West to try and save face.
But the North fights the South, what can I say
It will never make sense to my dying day.
What is this line that crosses the map,
It parts North from the South without any gap.

It's the 38th Parallel, so I am told,
There's a sign on the roadside upright and bold.
The next sign tells you dust can bring shells,
You look with a smile and think "what the hell".
They are telling you now that you are in view
By the enemy outpost that's looking for you.

They call this the Hook, I don't know why,
It's seen lots of battles light the night sky.
It's seen acts of courage, a thing to behold,
It's not for the weak, only the bold.
For this line is the place we have to defend,
For troops from the North it's their journey's end.

We fight for the South to help them stay free
From perils and hardships and yes tyranny.
For we are the soldiers of freedom they say,
We fight for the future not just for today.
We all did our duty with courage and pride,
From doing what's right we will never hide.

Roy (Brummy) Reece
Royal Army Medical Corps
26 Field Ambulance (No1 CCP)

A TRIP TO WAR

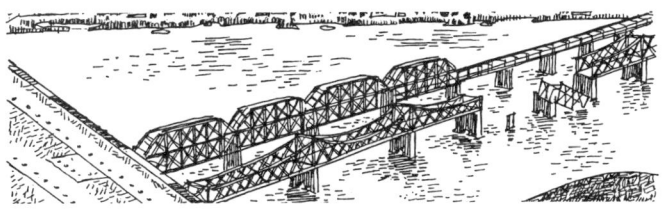

Service in North Africa, Tripoli and Tobruk,
As a boy, uncles fought here, they ran out of luck.
Soon in a troopship I'll sail from here,
Bound for a country that's called Korea.

Through the Suez, down the Red Sea,
Called in at Aden not a lot to see.
Then to Ceylon, now called Sri Lanka,
Troopship stops, out goes the anchor.

Few hours ashore we all go wild,
Plenty of tea, no bloody mild.
Indian Ocean then Singapore,
You'll do a route march, we did in a downpour.

On to Hong Kong, oh what a port,
It's ready and waiting, our armed escort.
Then on to Korea, a port called Pusan,
Wait for equipment, then up to the Han.

Over the Han all bridges blown,
Refugees in thousands, no home nothing to own.
It's summer, it's getting hot,
We hear later some were shot.

Up to the Imjin, I think of Blighty,
Dig in says the Sergeant, who's he God almighty.
Again and again I think of home,
But as a boy, the world I wanted to roam.

Here I am for maybe two years,
There'll be laughter, joy and a lot of tears.
Fear and terror, I'll often see red,
But if I go home I'll remember the dead.

Reg Briggs
Nan Troop Royal Signals,
attached 28th Field Regiment, Royal Engineers.

HELL'S HOLIDAY CAMP

(Haramura Battle School, Japan)

The tale I am about to tell
Is of the battle school of hell,
We started out all merry and bright, but at the station we had a fright,
For on the platform, we did see
With something shining on his sleeve,
A devil, with a harsh loud voice
It was, the Sergeant Major Joyce.

He formed us up in columns of three
We poor 'Norfolks' shook at the knees,
He gazed at us like a hungry shark, we found we were not here for a lark,
Then along the road we marched indeed
The Sergeant Major in the lead,
When at the camp we did arrive
We knew at once this was no skive.

As we marched through the gate
A band of instructors did await,
In their hands they held big sticks, as if they were performing tricks,
They stood there like a heap of goons
And split us into four platoons,
Then the instructors had their say
And moved us on our dismal way.

We stumbled through a wooden door
And dumped our kit on the dirty floor,
Then off we went to draw our beds, so that we could rest our weary heads,
No sheets or luxuries on our task
For that would be too much to ask,
Bur us 'Norfolks' we did not mind
We are fighting men, till two years' time.

When on parade a little later
A talk was given by the Mad Major,
We sat around him in the sun, then he had a little fun,
He told us if we did our best
We would get some well earned rest,
We tried our hardest but in vain
Only to be 'charged' again and again.

Then one day it came to pass
We ventured on our biggest task,
For five long days we did 'bang on', I'm sure we must have done it wrong,
Before the morn had broke
The Major with his stick did poke,
A little laddie in a trench
Smoking to his heart's content.

To the depot back we went
As all our bullets had been spent,
With 'Mad Major' in the lead, he returned the men of this happy breed,
We read our orders part one and two
And found we were in an awful stew,
For on the following Monday morn
Back to the 'Hell' camp at the crack of dawn.

As we common soldiers are
We travel distant and afar,
Leaving all good things behind
Nothing but blood, sweat and tears do we find.

A. R. (Tony) Sorrell
with the assistance of John Wigzell,
Ted Burrell and Private McCormack.
Royal Norfolks & Black Watch

THE BOYS IN BLUE

Who are these boys in Navy Blue? This rough unruly noisy crew,
Who sing and shout so late at night, who get so drunk, night after night.
Who are these men, the salt of the earth, what do they do,
what is their worth.
They'll walk the streets in fours and fives, haunting the pubs and lower dives.

I'll tell you about the boys in blue, where they come from and what they do.
I'll tell their story then you shall judge if you have a right their fun to grudge.
Our country homes seem so secure, the Army and Air Force there for sure
But these boys sail the ocean deep for days on end and seldom sleep.

These men know this in denim blue, their thoughts of England and of you.
For they know the Navy has no back door, they know the hazards twixt shore
and shore,
And so they sail the ocean waves knowing full well it might be their graves.
But still their watch they always keep upon all oceans oh so deep.

And then comes that time of day when all looks dismal, cold and grey
Which heralds the approaching night, when eyes are strained
and nerves grow tight.
And so these boys live for two weeks or three on that steel island far out at sea,
With never a comfort, just cold and damp, each man bewhiskered,
each man a tramp!

Often as well the food runs short whilst they search around still miles from port,
At such times as this they will have to make out on biscuits hard ore kye
or go without,
So now you folks will maybe see these boys are hardly like you or me.
That's why in port they must let go, whatever the impulse it's not just show.

So when you see them worse for drink, before you scorn them just
stop and think,
These boys may have just returned from hell, but if you ask them few will tell.
And British people will be free as long as our Navy
rules the sea.
Thank God, for these boys, though noisy true,
God bless them all, these boys in blue.

Ken Gordon, Royal Northumberland Fusiliers
who took passage on HMS Concord to Korea

THE LAND OF THE MORNING CALM

THE LAND OF THE MORNING CALM

Up the hill on sentry go.
The silver river down below
The sounds of night were all around.
Though dawn showed now, a paler blue.
That's when I sensed a change.
Something strange. Something new.
Among the trees. On dew wet grass.
I stood quite still, and listened hard.
Not a sound was there to hear.
No hoot, no croak, no rustle in the undergrowth.
The morning calm I came to know.
Up that hill on sentry go.
For all except my heart was still.
Then, without a whisper to explain.
It slipped away to whence it came.
To let each sound return anew.
Not until the morrows dawn did it come again.
Then, although prepared, I wondered still.
At the calm upon that hill.

Den Johnson
RAOC Section, attached 10th Infantry Workshops, REME

KOREA

Where the mighty ragged mountains rip the guts out of the sky,
And the desolation chills you to the marrow of your bones.
Where the blinding, drifting blizzards sear the unprotected eye,
And the biting bitter wind across the Yalu River moans.
A wild and savage landscape, with its valleys grim and dreary ...
Crag on wolfish crag, piled up, and glittering with the snows.
A harsh and brutal kingdom, that would make an angel weary...
But your Scottish Soldier fought there,
And he knows ... my God, he knows!

Ian E. Kaye
The Argyll and Sutherland Highlanders

OLD MOTHER-IN-LAW'S BREATH

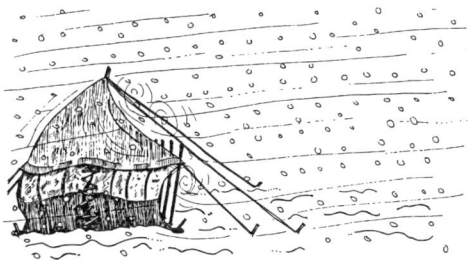

Far beyond the Yalu from the wastes of ice and snow,
The bitter wind comes howling from the north.
The cold is indescribable at thirty-five below
Conditions in which not to sally forth.
The biting air will numb the brain, and freeze the body fast,
Impossible to stand about for long.
Lest frostbite strikes you unawares amid the icy blast,
While keeping watch on some Korean 'dong'.

The vehicles were frozen too, their tyres stuck to the ground,
The antifreeze a solid block of ice.
While rations in each cardboard box, the greatest cook confound,
Yet somehow such materials sufficed.
The clothing we were issued with was really very good,
The 'parka' an especial source of joy.
It covered you from head to knee, and had a 'built-in' hood,
No wonder it was called "the real McCoy".

Korea is a cruel land - forget your 'Morning Calm' -
In winter fit for neither man nor beast.
And not the kind of climate where it pays to chance your arm -
Or someone might be calling for a priest.
Yet somehow we endured the cold - the ice and snow as well,
In spite of all the effort and the pain.
But best of all we beat that wind - that dreaded living hell -
That roared at us from some Manchurian plain.

W. A. (Tony) Thorn
1 King's Regiment (Liverpool)

MINUS FORTY

"All ranks are advised to breathe through the nose
and not the mouth to avoid frostbite of the lungs"

It's cold here in the mornings when we get up out of bed.
The washing water's frozen and there's frost upon my head.
The petrol fire is burning, but the atmosphere is chill,
Though the sun looks bleakly down upon our South Korean hill.

The snow that fell last year melted several days ago.
Now it's got much colder and it's far too cold to snow.
The winds that blow through China, south from dark Siberia,
Cut through our middle parkas and give us cause to fear.

First the water freezes and so does all the beer,
In the bottles, in the crates, in the NAAFI over here.
The margarine is solid; you can't spread it on your bread.
Your morning tea gets ice on if you wait until you're fed.

In the middle of the day, when the sun is overhead,
The temperature is freezing and then we start to dread,
How much colder can it get? Will it freeze us all to death,
In the middle of the night, with one great icy breath?

As the darkness comes again and the hills are blotted out
By the blackness of the winter, we really start to doubt
If it can be any colder any other place than hell;
If it will get any warmer after such a freezing spell.

While we sit here, round the fire, it's getting colder still,
On picket by the guard post for half an hour until
The next man 'out on stag' has to face the freezing night
Where the cold is like an enemy you don't know how to fight.

It gets colder, colder, colder, until you can't recall
Ever, never being cold, never ever warm at all.
We've got frostbite in our lungs and frostbite in our feet,
Frostbite in our fingers - like lumps of frozen meat.

In the east, between two hills, just above the sergeant's tent,
The morning light starts shining as another night is spent;
But it doesn't get much warmer as another day begins;
In fact, it's getting colder, I can feel it in my pins.

They say it's minus forty, and that's a lot of frost.
If you want it any colder you can go and get well lost.
I want to take my boots off and count my toes again;
(I've got two pairs of socks on) - I used to have all ten.

If I could just get warm again, or even really hot,
I should be so grateful, though I may sweat a lot.
For I shall not forget being cold as cold can be
With my teeth and eyeballs aching and as cold as charity.

John T. Boyd
Royal Signals, King Troop, 28 Brigade

DAWN VIGIL

The sky is blue, the mist, the dew,
The light, the haze, the day is new.

Whose mother's son, husband or brother,
Waits out there to set sight on another?

Far from his mind is my ill will,
But why be there if not to kill?

Some buddy's wit cuts through the air,
An answering call, his mate is still there.

Sh-h! The solitude, reluctant to break,
Someone dear is so near you ache.

Silence is music, just listen! You hear?
It may change its tune, though, and with it bring fear.

Your mucker whispers, you turn with a smile,
But he recently left us, isn't war vile?

To be alive is a luxury, so precious to keep,
Push from your mind those comrades who sleep.

The reverie fades, is allowed to drown,
As a familiar voice commands, "Right - Stand Down!"

Contributed by an anonymous friend of Peter Golding
Red Rose Branch BKVA

THE SKY OVER KOREA

I gaze at the sky and the sunrise
And see all the hilltops grow lighter.
I watch how the mist in the valley,
Retreats as the morning gets brighter.
The darkness that ruled the encampment
Gives way to the colours of the day;
To the reds and the blues and the yellows
And the clouds that are silver and grey.

I stare at those clouds and their patterns
That constantly break and reform;
Some looking like figures and faces
Of people I left back at home.
Why are heavens above us familiar
While the land that we walk on is strange?
Why do we belong to one country
If the air that we breathe doesn't change?

I gaze at the stars in the night time
And see something odd in the west.
The beam of a searchlight points upwards,
A symbol of man's peaceful quest.
The 38th parallel front line
Is neutral, just in that spot,
While the talks to decide on the future
Take place between them and our lot.

Perhaps we will all be united,
Or maybe we will fight to the death
In a country we've only just heard of
And where we may draw our last breath.
The moon and the stars shine above us
No matter wherever we stay,
And, though this is not our own country,
We'd better just live for today.

John T. Boyd
Royal Signals, King Troop, 28 Brigade

THEN AND FOREVER

I could always scent the river,
Feel the midnight ferries ride.
Steamers, tugs and liners too
Throbbing on the risen tide.

Always picture merchant-men
In from out the stinging storms
Looming up the Mersey channel
Making through the cold, damp morns.

But, below the quiet peasant
Humbles o'er his paddy fields.
Plods home his path in silence
'Fore the night to madness yields.

Up here, no friendly waters,
Surging staunchly to its sea.
Only dark, foreboding mountains,
Silent, threatening endlessly.

Terry Moore
The Royal Ulster Rifles

THE RAIN

The rain; obscuring distant hills.
The blinding rain - that soaks you through, and kills
The cooking-fires at birth.

The rain; that trickles coldly down your neck.
The pouring rain - the sodden kit, and mud that wrecks
A fighting-man's morale.

The rain: that soaks the soldier's bed.
The living rain - that patters gently on the dead,
And fills their eyes with tears.

The rain; that rusts the tanks and guns ...
The steady rain - that drips off tangled wire, and runs
In rivers, down the trench.

The rain; obliterating guardian flares.
The midnight rain - that makes the watchful sentry stare,
At silent shifting shadows.

The rain; never will you e'er forget,
The streaming rain - that foiled each hoarded cigarette,
And blurred the precious mail.

The rain; beats now on cosy cottage walls.
The friendly rain - that makes each one of us recall ...
But they who share the hearth know not!!

Ian E. Kaye
The Argyll and Sutherland Highlanders

THE PITY OF WAR

FLOTSAM ON THE TIDE

The flares - like flowers - bloomed
And lit the rainswept skies.
I saw the agony of Christ,
There in your patient eyes;
As you clutched your few possessions,
And made your way along,
The bloody, rutted mountain trail
To join the tragic throng.
You shuddered then, old man, with fear;
To hear the voice of Thor ...
As howitzers played their anthem
In the symphony of war!
No gentle peace and comfort
In the evening of your years,
Just the anguish of the journey
Thro' the lonely Vale of Tears.
You've shuffled-on thro' endless nights;
And days, of sleet and ice;
Burning your joss to Buddha,
And scrabbling for your rice.
Kith and kin, beyond your ken;
You know not where they lie ...
The "foreign devils" hurl their "birds"
Across your ancient skies!
You'll stagger-on, to God knows where -
It's eighty miles to Seoul!
If I were God, old man;
I'd take you from this world so cruel.
I'd place you with your ancestors,
On that mystic distant shore ...
Where the aged find contentment,
And an ever-open door.

Ian E. Kaye
The Argyll and Sutherland Highlanders

KOREAN DAWN

Grey dawn appears and heralds the sunrise.
The shapes of broken houses
show dark against the lightening sky.
From the rubble of blasted villages
shrouded forms of people rise
to search for loved ones
in the light of the silvery dawn.
Bomb blasted and derelict
the streets lie in ruinous array
with rescue parties struggling
in the first pale rays of sun.
Improvised stretchers move
back and forth and back again
as the injured are recovered and
the dead laid out in rows.
Day comes, and with it
the village throbs with the will of life
and people build anew.

Keith F. Thomson
Royal Electrical and Mechanical Engineers

SCARS OF WAR

The scars of war are there I find
Still rooted deep within my mind
Memories of those far off days
For me will never be erased.

The sight of children, faces blank
Orphaned by a shell or tank.
No one there to tend their need
But one young lady - shame indeed.

Someone must have left them there
Short of food and things to wear.
This little island with no name,
Was passed by time and time again.

As Christmas time was drawing near
To celebrate this time of year.
The Captain said: "We'll have a tree,
From that island there I see".

Not knowing there just out of view,
Were huts that housed this wretched few.
The children there were duly found,
Then as the word was passed around.

The crew sent food, clothing too
To help them all, that winter through.
Had we passed that island by,
Left those children there to die.

Who would have found the tragic scene
Where happy children once had been.
I now thank God we stopped that day
To help those children on their way.

When I think back, now I find
The children killed still haunt my mind.
I ask myself and always will,
How many did I help to kill.

Fred Kenrick
HMS Ceylon, Royal Navy

THE OLD MAN AND HIS COW

This incident happened in Korea in October 1951 after we had attacked a heavily defended hill. During this attack napalm bombs were used. We then advanced and occupied the hill. Our casualties were slight. Theirs were heavy. There was a village at the base of the hill, which had survived the napalm attack, and the road was choked with refugees streaming down from the north. It was a sad and terrible sight.

I stood by the empty hut
In an empty village,
With an empty heart,
And watched them come down from the north.
A walking flood of despairing humanity.
And I refused to allow
My heart to feel pity for them,
For if I had, I should have cried.

And soldiers are not supposed to cry!
They are trained fighting machines,
And machines do not cry.

I avoided their eyes,
Their accusing, resentful eyes,
And the air was electric with their unasked
Questions, that I could not answer.
But they cried.
Men, women and children, they cried.
But not me, for I was a soldier,
And soldiers do not cry.

Besides, it was not my home
That was about to be destroyed!
It was not my country that was torn in half!
Why should I cry for them?
Would any of them have volunteered, as I did, to
Go ten thousand miles away to fight for my home?
My country? Me?

And still they came on,
Choking the road with their life.
Heading South to freedom,
And a shanty village where only the rats were well fed!

And when thay had passed, and we were alone,
We fired the village.
Obeying orders, as good soldiers should.
'Leave nothing the enemy can use …!'
That was the order we dared not refuse.

And as I helped to burn their homes
I did not cry.
For I was a soldier, and soldiers do not cry.

Then we found them!
The old man and his cow.
They had been hiding in some bushes,
And when we found them he was crying, bitterly!

The enemy had killed his family.
They had plundered his home.
Ravaged his village.
Leaving him nothing except his cow.
And our orders were,
'Leave nothing the enemy can use!'
Not even a cow!

We looked at the old man. He looked at us.
We looked at the cow.
And the old man cried.

But I did not cry.
For I was a soldier, and soldiers do not cry.

'Leave nothing the enemy can use'
That was the order we dared not refuse.

Still the old man cried.
He had seen what the enemy could do.
He had seen his family killed.
Now we were burning his home, his village,
Leaving him nothing …
But his cow …?

An officer gave an order. Two men carried it out!
One took hold of the old man, and led him away.
The other took the cow, and led it away.
The old man did not resist, or struggle.
He simply cried.

'Leave nothing the enemy can use.'
That was the order we dared not refuse.
Not even a cow!

The order was carried out.
To the letter.
In moments it was done.
Strong, willing hands picked up the cow,
And placed her safely in a truck.

And the old man cried.
But differently now
As they placed him in the truck
Beside his cow!

The truck drove south,
Leaving nothing the enemy could use.
Not even a cow!

Who says soldiers don't cry?

Not I!
Not I ...!

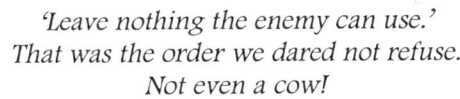

Denis J. Woods
45 Field Regiment and 20 Field Regiment RA

SOLDIER TO SOLDIER

Who were you Jack - who lie there sprawled upon your back?
What then that struck ... and hurled your youthful manhood
In the muck, of fields so bleak as these?
The blood is fresh upon your cheeks,
And bone protrudes from shattered knees.

Your death-grip tight, around the rifle's battered sights ...
Equipment shrapnel-torn; for this day, Laddie, were you born
In homely Scottish shire!
Here you lie; the tanks race by, and spray your mangled form with mire.

Your eyes are clear! For a dead man's eyes that's bloody queer.
You poor young sod!
Perhaps you see the pathway up to God ...
The last Parade of all ...
I see your tattered bonnet, hanging on the dug-out wall.

Your Spirit's gone: your corpse casts grotesque shadows in the sun.
We are but dust. I see your rifle number, faintly, thro' the rust.
You feel no pain; nor sigh ... There goes the call:
We're moving up ... I leave you as you lie!
Farewell!!

Ian E. Kaye
The Argyll and Sutherland Highlanders

IN THE LINE

THE MORNING CALM

As the first streaks of dawn
Herald the approaching day,
They paint the gaunt black mountains against the lightening sky.

The radio man calls an air strike in
Adding noise to battlefield din,
All is fair in the beastliness of war, air power is the equation to win.

F86 Silver Sabres swoop
Dropping pods of destruction,
Burns all in its path, indiscriminate in its corruption.

The bloody plain below reveals
The carnage wrought,
With twisted inert men, scattered, laying where they fought.

Soil churned to a quagmire
From shell, bomb and mortar,
Shattered tanks trapped in mud, dying men cry for water.

The clatter of choppers,
Medics save whoever they may be,
Then off to the USS Haven, anchored safely at sea.

The young men sent to fight here
For a political cause,
Curse the politicians as they stare into death's jaws.

They would rather be at home
With their family and friends,
Than lie buried here on foreign soil for eternity's ends.

Let those who have fallen for freedom
Lie in silence and peace,
And our politicians who preach democracy, remember - at least.

Colin Fowles
Inchon Korea, 16th September 1950

THE MORNING CALM

The pre-dawn hour - STAND TO!
Enter the communication trench
to the forward slope fighting trenches,
greet your mates with the usual muttered ribald profanities.

Identify the dark clumps to your front
that you know should be there.
All patrols are 'home' - if anything moves it is not one of us..

Begin the silent vigil
fine-tune hearing and sight
hoping you see nothing, hear nothing out of place.
"At home - it is the evening of the night we have already had
- living our lives ahead of theirs".

All is profoundly still
the sky-line stealthily lightens with the first blush
- see your breath condensing in the rarified gloaming.

The star that lights our day raises its rim
- as if by magic a veil the breadth of the sky is lifted
and The Land of the Morning Calm is revealed.

Truly it is breathtakingly beautiful
- only rendered ugly by what might lurk fathoms below its mantle.

Hill-tops can be seen - our front line - and theirs -
each hill-top fort garrisoned with defenders
'standing-to' to repel the threat of invaders.

Dozens, hundreds of islands to the horizon
- the incredible Morning Calm sea surrounding.

The Morning Calm sea married to incorporeal calm acoustic
the intense deadening sound of nothingness
- eerie essence of calmness.

The radiant golden orb drives away the mist
- ethereal at the edges where it laps the island shores,
more and more land is exposed
soon all is gone burnt off by the brazen sun
and its promise of another scorching day.

All is as it should be
- STAND DOWN!

Peter Fisher
The King's Shropshire Light Infantry

I HAVE!

Have you known the lonely silence …
Not a bird-or-bug is stirring?
Your 'Mucker' lies there snoring
In his blankets at your side.
The dew drips off the Bren gun …
You can hear the damp grass growing;
And each squeak of your equipment
Is thunder, magnified!

Have you known the lonely silence …
At the witching-hour of midnight?
You've patted each grenade ten times,
And even whispered to your Sten …
Dozed-off - then woke in panic
With the fear of death upon you,
And every shape and shadow seems
Chock-full of 'little men'!

Have you known the lonely silence …
In the hour before the 'Stand-to'?
When every nerve is screaming
That there's Enemy around …
Then let your mess tins rattle,
Like a herd of berserk cattle …
Or stood and coughed (with hair on end!)
And shuddered at the sound?
I have!

Ian E. Kaye
The Argyll and Sutherland Highlanders

YONG DONG

Yellow grass rustles in the disputed valley.
On our left 'The Hook', illuminated by twinkling flares.
Nothing to report.
Going on to Manchester, looming ahead in the moonlit distance.

Droplets of sweat sting our eyes,
As we strain to pierce the shadowy darkness.
Ominous sounds drift on the humid air,
From across the swollen Samichon.
Night will soon creep into misty dawn but
Golden moon and silver stars still dimly light the course that we must take.

Ken Cornwell
The Durham Light Infantry

TO A PATROL ON 355

Towering bulk, silhouetted against an Asian moon.
Huddled in bunkers, flinching with each explosion.
Rivulets of sweat streak the young tensed faces.
Every man too scared to show his fear,
Every man an island with his thoughts.

Fifteen selected for this patrol,
Into paddy fields hard frozen by the arctic blast.
Venturing into that desolate wasteland.
Expecting the worst, hoping for redemption.

Fire fight reported on the 88.
In the CP the CO waits, concern etched upon his soldier's face.
Very lights arc into the frosty air.
Even the stars are trembling.

Ken Cornwell
The Durham Light Infantry

KOREAN INCIDENT

The moon hangs low, above the snow-capped peaks.
A sentry stamps the feet he cannot feel ...
A nervous cough re-echoes o'er the snow, and
Moonbeams dance upon the burnished steel.
Beyond the wire, the frozen paddies gleam:
A burnt-out tank plays tricks with tired eyes ...
Warning flares transform the bitter night -
The enemy is flushed from where he lies!
In haste, the warriors tumble from their beds,
To man the trenches gained at bloody cost ...
'Twixt Sten and Bren, the luckless try to flee;
They give their scarlet blood into the frost:
And all is still! "Stand Down", the order goes -
The man on "Stag" ... begins to feel his toes!

Ian E. Kaye
The Argyll and Sutherland Highlanders

AQUILA NON CAPIT MUSCAS:
The Eagle Does Not Catch Flies

The eagle does not catch flies!
But, have you seen the flies when the eagle dies?
Fly-blown Fusiliers that the maggots eat;
No cool, English graveyard for them in their defeat.

In endless monotone they orchestrate; in curiosity and industry;
From living tissue to the dead; from the vomit of the dying and
The faeces soldier-made; on impulse, flitting from the food we eat;
Inextricably attracted by dead and living things.

I pray to God that it is winter when I die! If not,
Bury me that day; leave me not in death sine die;
For mercy's sake, bury me before the stench arrives;
Leave not my once worn eagle's body to the flies!

Ashley Cunningham-Boothe
The Royal Northumberland Fusiliers

KEEP IT QUIET

Written after my first experience of an ambush patrol. The equally nervous patrol leader constantly urging us to 'Keep it Quiet'.

Ambush patrol, and it's my turn.
Assembled at the mine gap,
Weapons checked, radio tested.
Someone coughs.
Keep it quiet.

He stands beside me in the narrow trench,
Sweating more than I.
Bren gun on safety, waiting for the word.
Right let's go.
Keep it quiet.

The moon dodging from cloud to cloud,
Or so it seems to my apprehensive eye.
Frosted breath rising into the frozen air.
Ice sheeted paddy crunching beneath our boots.
Keep it quiet.

Here's the place.
Take position by the paddy bank,
Grass obscuring our field of fire.
Call Big Sunray on the 88
Keep it quiet.

A falling flare lights up the scene.
Bushes seem to move in the silvery glow.
Nothing there.
Fifteen heads rise slowly once again.
Keep it quiet.

Movement to the left.
Something rustles in the frozen grass.
All feeling gone from feet and fingers.
Call Control, it's time to go.
Keep it quiet.

Ken Cornwell
The Durham Light Infantry

A LETTER HOME

During my service in Korea with 64 Field Park Squadron, Royal Engineers, one of my friends was Sapper Robbie Lancaster who came from Attleborough near Norwich. Robbie would recite poems he had written in the form of letters to his mother, or imaginary letters he had received from home, to cheer us all up. I have kept the following poem in my service pay book for over forty years.

Paul Harriott, 64 Field Park Squadron, Royal Engineers

Dear Mum, it seems like ages since we came over here
To battle on for glory in this land they call Korea.
I've had time to settle in, the time to look around,
I've had the time to leave my mark upon the battleground.
But Mum it's hard to battle on, it's hard to make a show,
When you're frozen to the marrow and you're slipping in the snow.

Where your muckers all around you are dropping off like flies,
And the blindness comes to get you from the snow glare in your eyes.
The grub is always frozen and your head is full of lice,
While the water in your bottle is a solid lump of ice.
When you grab your gun to fire it at some advancing Chink,
The steel it leaves a blister, well it kind of makes you think.

Oh to be in England where there's heat enough to share,
And the lovely dancing sunbeams cast a warmth into the air.
Where a man can live in comfort and find a helping hand,
I would give a lot to be there in my blessed native land.
With the sound of water tinkling in a quiet woodland dell,
Takes the place of banzai screaming which knocks your nerves to hell.

Bur first there is this war to win, to make our homeland free,
To make this world around us like one big family.
So I'll spit upon my bayonet and prime a new grenade,
And never let those Communists ever think that I'm afraid.
Oh to hope that I'll be good enough to see this job well done,
I'm sending you this letter
from your ever loving son.

Robbie Lancaster
64 Field Park Squadron, Royal Engineers

GOT YOUR MAIL

Cold tonight maybe thirty below
Shivering ... teeth chattering ... hope there's no snow
Feet stuck in ice in this terrible trench
No smell of death tho' I remember its stench.

It's still, so still, moon's coming out
We're on standby, whisper don't shout
A look at my mate, makes me feel better
Oh John, did you get your letter?

Reliefs arrive, passwords exchanged, no enemy yet, too bloody cold
Get to the rear, the orders are told
Make a hot brew, there might be tinned stew
See Yehudi and Saul - think they are Jews.

Mail got through, came from HQ
One for your mate, none for you
Mate looks pale and really glum
Be months before we get warm sun.

Full kit on we try and sleep
Guns and ammo all in a heap
Mate's gone outside with his gun, tin hat on
Bang, shot through the head ... he'd read his Dear John.

Reg Briggs
Nan Troop Royal Signals,
attached 28th Field Regiment Royal Engineers

WIRELESS OPERATOR

How many wearied hours, how many days between?
Two worlds - strangely alone
They stumble up the mountain ways
Talking into their microphone.
These trumpeters of modern wars
Whose calls transcend the skies and ring
About the un-numbered corridors
And down their starlit wandering.
For many faithful friend unseen
They garner in the urgent news.
Something that was or should have been
Theirs is to echo - not to choose.
Theirs too, to echo some forlorn
And hard-pressed ally's call for aid:
This from some distant hill is drawn
The tumult of another blade.
Not for these men the quiet relief
Of speeding help to their distress.
'Thanksgiving' throws a dice with 'grief',
While these alternatively press
Against their tired obedient ears
The salt of other people's tears.

Kilroy of Nottingham

THE RADIO OPERATOR

Top of the mountain ... above the cloud
Below, sounds of battle, so very loud.
Crackle of the radio, message relayed..
Will the enemy find me. Hope not, I've prayed.

Hide yourself, and set, by day
Will the enemy come this way
Clouds cleared now, I take a deep breath
Below men, guns, tanks and death.

It's night again, I'm cold and wet
My duty is to man the set
Earphones on Morse code I hear
Not one message gives me cheer.

Crump, crump mortar bombs land near
I'm OK so is my gear
Another message, this time in code
Ammo, stores received ... but only half load

I think of home so far away
Will I live another day
What's that noise ... I tremble with fear
Is it the enemy, are they near.

Get down low you can't be seen
Oh for a bath, oh to be clean
Safety catch off, ready to fire
Then they pass ... they missed the trip wire.

I'm proud of my trade and regiment
Anywhere in the world I can be sent
I operate on land, on sea and in the air
In war and peace I will be there.

Reg Briggs
Nan Troop Royal Signals,
attached 28th Field Regiment Royal Engineers

THE SNIPER

Oh, God!
Now sits a man within my sights.
He's smiling and relaxed, at leisure.
Sublimely unaware that his frail life
Lies solely within my pleasure.

He sits in sun and waffles on,
No doubt regaling his friends and cronies
With the rights and wrongs of army life
And denouncing all officers as phonies.

By what right do I have this power?
What right to make such a God-like decision?
One squeeze and I can destroy this man:
Snuff him out with no chance of revision.

What crazy duty demands that I should kill
Some poor Gook who doesn't remotely matter?
If I shoot the poor sod, news of my success
Would scarce interrupt company chatter?

So it's safety catch on and rifle to rest,
My softness acknowledge with a profanity,
Yet inwardly I rejoice and have peace of mind,
Knowing I've retained my humanity.

Douglas John Hollands
1st Battalion The Duke of Wellington's Regiment

A LOST FRIEND

Today I lost a good friend
A loss time will never mend.
He was only nineteen,
Tall, hungry and lean

But a bullet went straight through his brain

Today I lost a good friend
So shy he would never offend.
No one considered him clever
But we all admired his endeavour

But a bullet went straight through his brain

Today I lost a good friend.
A lad on whom I could depend.
We once picked up a young pro
And he gave me first go

Truly the mark of a friend!

Douglas John Hollands
1st Battalion The Duke of Wellington's Regiment

SONG OF A BIRD

Upon a frozen ridge, one winter's day,
An army chaplain knelt, and tried to pray.
But somehow, his tongue knew not the word ...
Instead, he found his weary mind listening - to a bird!

Just a tiny tuft of feathers, in a tree.
A little heart, brimful of ecstasy!
The song it sang, so wonderfully sweet ...
Echoed across the valley, at the tired - Padre's feet.

He listened there, entranced, as in a dream.
Outlined: kneeling, in the sunlight's gleam.
Each joyous note, that pealed in such a flood ...
Uplifted him. He smiled, and knew the
- Master understood!

Ian E. Kaye
The Argyll and Sutherland Highlanders

A WORTHLESS HILL

Dawn is nigh, when it comes, they will come!
Am I to see tomorrow's dawn? Feel tomorrow's sun?
Yonder appears the first pale streaks of light!
Is this to be my last day? Was that my last night?

Last night, filled with sound, a night of fear,
Rising to a crescendo, now dawn is near.
Tuneless bugles, crashing symbols, a hideous sound.
Am I to die here, for this worthless mound?

This worthless mound that war's laid bare.
What are they like, those strangers out there?
Do they sweat with fear, as they wait to kill?
Wait to kill or die, on this worthless hill.

This is not my war! Not my dear land!
Why have I been guided here by fate's cruel hand?
For my country, my loved ones, I'd willingly die!
Is this the foreign soil where my body will lie?

Now I can see him, my fellow being.
Daylight has sent the last shadows fleeing.
A grey clad multitude has appeared into view.
'Dear God! They are so many! We so few...'

'Look to your front!' A calm voice rings out.
So this is what war is all about.
'Pick out your targets!' Fire at will!'
Is this where life ends, on a Korean hill ... ?

Roy Carswell
Kings Shropshire Light Infantry

I'LL COME TO NO HARM

Korea "Land of the Morning Calm"
A peaceful country, a divided country
A country at war, I'll come to no harm.

Left school at fourteen, sixteen the Army
Eighteen volunteered for war family said "He's barmy".
I'll come to no harm.

Still a boy with a lot to learn
Is this war really my concern
I'll come to no harm.

Nineteen today, in a killing zone
Been frightened … scared … but I'll not moan
I'll come to no harm.

Comrades missing, wounded. Killed by shell
This place is hell
I'll come to no harm.

Something I saw - it wasn't nice
Refugees placing babies under ice
I'll come to no harm.

I'm twenty now, I've learnt a lot
In winter it's cold, summer it's hot
I'll come to no harm.

At times we stink, it's then I think
I might not go home, mate gives me a wink
I'll come to no harm.

Two years up, I'm at a loss
Going home, I came to no harm
For all the time out here, I carried a cross.

In later years I often shed tears
Comrades dead, with them no more beers.
At least I know they'll come to no harm.

Reg Briggs
Nan Troop Royal Signals, attached 28th Field Regiment RE

THE BARLEY MOW

A poem written whilst in PoW Camp No.1. It puts in perspective the type of food which we were given in the early days of incarceration in the PoW camp. The food consisted of - millet seed, sorghum seed and polluted rice, richly endowed with white maggots, the whole lot was served as a gruel cooked up in a great cast iron open cooking pot with a huge wooden lid. Most of the PoWs had rusty but well used "K" ration tins mostly picked up from old battle areas that we passed through on our way north to the designated PoW camps. It paid to have a large tin as your rations would fit into it comfortably; unfortunately, if you had a one pound tin you didn't get your whole ration and there was no going back for seconds - it was one meal a day!

At the beginning the Chinese interpreters dished out the meal and we were not allowed to eat until they blew the whistle - one blast to commence, two to stop. Later they let us British set up our own cookhouse and nominate our own cooks and servers; this I must say was a very sought after job, which wasn't relinquished gladly; after all hunger was one of the worst enemies besides the Chinese that we had to endure. The above state of affairs lasted for about the first fifteen months of our captivity, then because of the high death rate among PoWs (mostly our American comrades) and the necessity to have enough PoWs to barter with at Panmunjon, the situation began to improve. These improvements accelerated toward the end, especially the last six months, as our captors wanted us to look fat and well cared for at the repatriation point, instead of the pathetic skeletons we had been through their neglect and indifference, both medically and physically a year earlier. So many need not have perished had the Chinese adhered to the Geneva Convention, which as you know they did not recognise.

Seated one day with my barley wishing it were bread and cheese,
I put my bowl of barley down between my knees
I waited for the whistle which was for us to start
When I took a spoon a bit too soon and heard a voice remark,
You cannot start yet student the whistle hasn't blown,
You must all start together remember you're not at home,
This is our lenient policy which means fair shares for all,
So let us start together or slow eaters get sod all.

I heard the whistle blowing and stood up there with grace,
The whistle then was blown again and so commenced the race,
You never saw such a sight before it was a real disgrace,
Some silly sods missed their gobs and slapped it in their face,
At last I cleaned my bowl and dashed out for some more,
I thought I was the first one but some got there before,
It was a proper scramble lads just like a rugby scrum,
I worked my way right to the bin to find that there was none.

Now here's the moral of my story: if there's not much in the bin,
When you're first for chop-chop take a whacking great 7lb tin.

The reason for dashing back to the rice pot outlined in the poem, was that the remaining rice sludge burnt to the bottom and sides of the pot, resulting in flakes of thick burnt rice which were quite delectable indeed in our state at the time, and considered as good as candy.

William Gibson
The Royal Ulster Rifles

THE KOREAN ENCOUNTER

The year was nineteen hundred and fifty-one,
I said to myself "What have I done"
For along with many I felt some fear
As we sailed to War out in Korea

On board our ship the Sergeant said
"Pay attention lads, or you'll soon be dead"
The weather out there is very cold
Don't get frostbite, you've been told
If you get cut off and you're all alone
Whatever you do don't think of home
Make sure your gun has one up the spout
For if the enemy sees you, it's no use to shout."

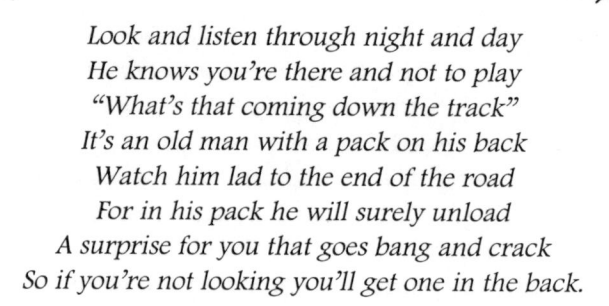

Look and listen through night and day
He knows you're there and not to play
"What's that coming down the track"
It's an old man with a pack on his back
Watch him lad to the end of the road
For in his pack he will surely unload
A surprise for you that goes bang and crack
So if you're not looking you'll get one in the back.

"Hi buddy" called a visiting Yank
"Do you mind if I look over your tank"
"Hey, for a bottle of beer you can have my Jeep"
"Sure take it away, it's yours to keep"

It's snowing hard very cold and wet
It's Christmas Day, one I'll never forget
No time for yearning, there's a job to do
With a bit of luck it will soon be through
As I look at the hills that straight ahead lie
To be retaken once more, with so many to die
We wonder a lot when the end will be
To stop this stupid insanity.

Can't be long now for my "R & R break"
"Gee, a pint of beer down by the lake
This Tokyo is a wonderful city
The food is good, and the girls so pretty
It's not long you can guess for the time to go back
To the place they call home in the ground
Yes once more we're Korea bound.

Your 'tour' is now over and you pack your mess-can,
And go hell for leather down south to Pusan.
When you get home and you're back in your chair
You'll have plenty of time to sit and stare
To think of those killed; of many you knew
Just thank God - it could have been you!

Bert Hutchings
5th Royal Inniskilling Dragoon Guards

COMMISSION IN KOREA

I served out in Korea on HMS Ceylon
That was nineteen fifty
Oh where has that time gone
For I was then a young man
The crew mostly young men too
Two Captains bold but very old
That was the general view
Ships from many Nations served in Korea too
Out on patrol, so very cold
Different flags they flew
But one was common to us all
United Nations Blue
Up and down the coast we went
The charts we used weren't new
That would have caused some washing
Had it been leaked to the crew
The occasional trip to the tip
Of an island that we knew
To stretch our limbs dive and swim
See sights that were new
A bottle of two of English brew
Would signal we were through
Then back onboard not quite so bored
To start patrols anew, we'd stalk our foe
So we could throw a six inch shell or two
About two years this lasted
I think that we all knew
The old ship she was knackered
And we were knackered too
At last the signal came
To cease that life we knew
Then go ashore in Singapore
Where the ship was made brand new
The Vengeance which was Portsmouth bound
Took home the weary crew
So ends Ceylon's commission in nineteen fifty two.

Fred Kenrick
The Royal Navy (HMS Ceylon)

THE HOOK

A hill stands in Korea they named it the Hook,
You won't find it on a map or in a guide book.
It stood dark against the sky, a place men went to die.
Men blanched at the mention of its name,
Prayed they'd never have to go there again.
Just half a mile of trenches and barbed wire.

No colour to be seen
Only shell holes where the grass had been.
No animals, no birds, no grass or trees,
No springs flowed down to the paddy fields below.
The hill looked like the landscape on the moon
Craters covered the ground from shells falling all around.

Shells fell like raindrops, morning, noon and night,
From enemy guns hidden well out of sight.
Men in sandbag bunkers hid away
As shells exploded every minute of the day.
The roofs shook above their heads,
While earth fell and covered all their beds.

Shell blasts came rushing in through the door,
Laying a blanket of sand on the floor.
The ground shook beneath their feet,
As their Maker they prepared to meet.
In daylight nothing moved, only shrapnel filled the air
From exploding shells landing there.

As darkness fell like rats they crept,
Down the trench armed to the teeth,
Lifted the wire and crawled underneath,
Down the hill and on to the track,
With bren guns heavy on their back,
Every step brought danger and a rifle's crack.

Fear of a flare illuminating the night,
While they stood statue like, exposed in the light,
Fear of the cold black fog rolling up the valley,
In 30 degrees of frost, unwise to dally.
Yet they lay waiting for the enemy to show,
In the bitter cold, frost and snow.

They waited six hours or more, jumping at every sound,
Eyes red with lack of sleep warily scanning the ground.
At first light six frozen bodies crossed the valley,
To get home before daylight with only one desire,
For a hot drink and a warm fire,
Up the hill till they came to the wire.

Their blackened faces shone in the weak sunlight,
But any resemblance to men had taken flight,
Like zombies up the trench they crept.
Once inside the bunker more shells began to fall,
As they cowered fully clothed against the smoke black wall,
They dropped on to their make-shift beds and then oblivion.

Shells were falling, the ground ran red,
With the blood of the wounded and the dead.
Bunker after bunker collapsed,
Shelling and bombing throughout the day,
When they woke only holes could be seen,
Where hours ago bunkers had been.

Barbed wire blasted into weird shapes pointed skywards.
Posts twisted like corkscrews still stood tall
Others were embedded in the trench wall.
The once straight trench twisted like a snake
The sandbag walls collapsing was more than they could take.
Shreds of sandbags hung on the barbed wire.

Smoke and stench drifts in the breeze,
But with daylight fading, once more they had to go
On another patrol in the valley below.
Another night of hell out in the snow,
So on and on it went, winter turned to summer,
The guns fell silent, it was the end of the Korean War.

At last it was all over, shelling no more.
They walked away from that hill and counted the cost,
The wounded, the dead and the soldiers lost.
We never went back to the Hook but the memories linger.
The men who fought there everyone a hero to me
And forever will stay in my memory.

D. Miller
The Duke of Wellington's Regiment

The British losses on the Hook between 10-29 May 1953 amounted to 219, of these 176 were soldiers of The Duke of Wellington's Regiment.

THE SAGA OF THE COMUS

Once off Inchon, Korea way,
The Comus patrolled one sunny day
Suddenly there was a ruddy big bang,
As two Yaks did a wizard prang.

Old horseface Palmer on the bridge
Said they can't be ours, they must be Migs
It made the Skipper curse and swear
To see old horseface standing there.

The "gunner I" in the after flat
Was suddenly knocked upon his back
As "Buck Taylor" came charging thro,
Knowing he had a job to do.

Nicholson on the "director sight"
Couldn't find the stop, so got a fright,
For the starboard single made a leap.
It was enough to make you weep.

Buck Taylor on the starboard gun,
Was very nearly made to run,
One of the Yaks went Phut! Phut!
And put a cannon shell right by his foot.

"Dizzy Mason" on the "Iron Deck"
Shrapnel in the chest and neck
Staggered to the W.T.
There was told we are too busy.

Went on to the forward Mess
To try and get some goddamned rest
Moaned and groaned and said "Ee bah gum"
I wish they'd send me home to mum.

Tingerling by the galley door
Suddenly went on a flying tour
Showed up later on the after gun
Black as a nigger, so caused some fun.

Addison, in the No.1 boiler room,
Suddenly came to meet his doom
When the water came rushing in,
There was no way of saving him

His passing will not be in vain,
And memory will long remain,
And a roll of honour in St Paul's
A plaque of granite in the wall.

The names of all British Korean dead,
And a sacred book will be read,
So sleep on friend in Valhalla Hall,
Forever remembered by shipmates all,
We will remember him. Amen.

Buck Taylor
The Royal Navy, HMS Comus

END OF THE JOURNEY

"What's the matter with the light?"
The Nurse quietly stood by his bed.
"I can't see very well, tonight ... Mother; where is Ted? ...

The Major says a dawn attack ...
Sure, Mum, I'll wear my coat.
I'll get a letter soon I guess ... Nurse! Oh, Nurse! My throat ...

Daphne, darling; sure we will,
Just as soon as I get back ...
Rotten luck! Poor bastard, copped a burst; right in the back ...

Sorry! Can't make the Game today ...
Frank! They're coming down the trench!!!
Aw, Dad! Who plonked his muddy rugger boots right on my bench? ...

Mum! ... Please hold my hands again ..."
And the young Nurse softly cried ...
She held his hands; and her hot tears flowed,
As the lonely soldier died. ("Stand Easy!")

Ian E. Kaye
The Argyll and Sutherland Highlanders

ON HEARING NEWS OF THE ARMISTICE

On the day the armistice was signed,
And the old front line vacated.
When Mao and Kim had cause to laugh
Their warlike appetites now sated;
A Tommy lay in hospital
With a plate inside his head,
And the paper he was reading
Most informatively said
That the cost of war to North Korea
Must be a billion sterling,
Is it any wonder now
That his poor brain was whirling?
He scratched his head so hard it bled,
He didn't notice t'bleeding,
As more surprises met his eyes
He just continued reading.
The author of the article,
Declared a little later,
That the total cost to Britain
Was considerably greater.
Each UN country, in its turn,
Was carefully dissected,
The cost increased in everyone,
'Twas not what he expected.
With anger and bewilderment,
He stared in shocked surprise,
He gave his shattered legs a thump
Then shouted to the skies;
"Don't know how we got in this war;
I don't care who begun it;
But what I'd damned well like to know
Is who the hell has won it?"

Ken Cornwell
The Durham Light Infantry

IRREVERENT

POSTED TO THE P.B.I.

Infantrymen we are now, my boys.
Foot sloggers doomed to crawl on our bellies.
Proudly we march under new colours,
Part of the Duke of Wellies.
The West Riding is our new home
A fine county that inspires traditions.
Yorkshiremen all, sturdy and tall,
Born and bred into fighting conditions.

Dukes, Dukes we are now, my boys
Bloody and heroic is our story.
Tommy Atkins was one of us, my boys,
So ours to enhance his glory.

Halifax is our base. God what a place!
With barracks like an old prison,
It's a town of flat caps, bombed-out gaps
And young tarts who're hardly a vision.
In alleys they lurk, half hidden in murk,
Each one poised like a painted vulture.
The lads love 'em all, screw 'em agin a wall,
Then boast proudly of Halifax culture

Dukes, Dukes we are now, my boys
Bloody and heroic is our story.
Tommy Atkins was one of us, my boys,
So ours to enhance his glory.

We're chased half to death, with no time for breath,
But at training we get better and better,
Then as night closes in we go looking for sin
With old Foggy always our go-getter.
With girls hardly shy and beer in good supply
We take 'em cheap and in deep measure.
But defying the MPs, with consummmate ease,
Is always our greatest pleasure.

Dukes, Dukes we are now, my boys
Bloody and heroic is our story.
Tommy Atkins was one of us, my boys,
So ours to enhance his glory.

Then the inevitable comes: the War Office (the bums)
Send us an embarkation order.
The comfort of whores and days on the moors,
Are to be replaced by a Commie Marauder.
For Korea we're bound, where nothing is found
But death and horrific mutilations.
Where civil strife rules, we're the poor fools,
Who'll fight as the United Nations.

Dukes, Dukes we are now, my boys
Bloody and heroic is our story.
Tommy Atkins was one of us, my boys,
So ours to enhance his glory.

At Soton we debus, with a minimum of fuss,
Our voices raised in songs ribald and bawdy.
Bunting is flying and relatives are crying,
With the old Trooper standing there all gaudy.
A parting at sea is a new one on me
And fresh thoughts of death are distressing.
But why give a damn, fool that I am!
Hasn't the Padre given us his blessing?

Dukes, Dukes we are now, my boys
Bloody and heroic is our story.
Tommy Atkins was one of us, my boys,
So ours to enhance his glory.

Douglas John Hollands
The Duke of Wellington's Regiment

FOLLOW THE LEADER

If you should be invited to go out on a patrol,
Into the frozen paddy fields below
You are perfectly entitled fore you go upon that stroll
To hear some things you really ought to know.

If your leader is a Major it will add a little spice,
He'll have seen it all before, you must agree.
He'll lead you out and back again as quiet as little mice;
'Cause he's thinking of those Colonel's pips, you see.

A Captain as your leader should fill you with concern.
He'll take no heed of either you or me.
If he's going to be promoted he's still got a bit to learn,
And he's bound to want to win his first VC.

A Lieutenant may prove safer, so I'm told by the old hands.
He'll tell to err t'wards caution if there's trouble.
A patrol led by a 'Louie' will undoubtedly come through,
And if you bump em then you'll get back at the double.

A 'Single Pipper' never shirks his task, I understand.
So help him all you can on your joint mission,
But beware my friend and never ever try to hold his hand.
We'd hate the Chinks to get the wrong impression.

The safest bet's the CSM (a credit to your mob)
His plans reveal his gift for pure invention.
A patrol led by our Harry will always do the job
And you'll be heroes when you aint the least intention.

So now you erstwhile squaddies you've heard all you need to know
Just remember all the advice given here.
Please choose your leader carefully, and keep your heads down low,
Then you'll be around for more patrols next year.

Ken Cornwell
The Durham Light Infantry

NOT ME SIR!

Yes Sir, no Sir, three bags full Sir,
Right turn, left turn, loads of bull Sir,
Blanco, brasso, four-by-two Sir
Sten gun, bren gun, rifle too Sir!

Mayday, payday shining boots Sir,
Right wheel, left wheel, halt, salute, Sir,
Cap badge straight in beret blue Sir,
Tax deductions, sports fund too Sir?

Nig-nogs marching count two-three Sir,
Guards and pickets, NAAFI tea Sir,
Eyes right, eyes left, marching feet Sir,
Two on, four off, in this heat Sir?

Big pack, small pack, webbing belt Sir,
Greatcoat, gloves and snowballs melt Sir,
B.D. blouse box-pleats look smart Sir,
Paybook, first and second part Sir!

Lance-jack, corporal, sergeants stripes Sir,
Lanyards, puttees - gaiter-type Sir.
Foreign posting's just come through Sir
Embarkation leave is due Sir!

Troopships, drafting, far-off shores Sir,
Jungle greens drawn from the stores Sir,
Cookhouse duties, soaking wet Sir,
Monsoon rain, mosquito net Sir!

Written to my next-of-kin Sir,
Been abroad to get some in Sir,
Flashes on my arm bequest Sir,
Campaign medals on my chest Sir!

Twenty one and twenty two Sir,
Group number will soon be due Sir,
Early breakfast, then goodbye Sir,
Civvy street and flashy tie Sir!

Two years go so very quick Sir,
Army life is not my pick Sir,
Settle down and take a wife Sir,
Steady job, set up for life Sir!

John T. Boyd
Royal Signals, King Troop, 28 Brigade

ADVICE TO AN OFFICER

We Tommies at the front suffer, sir.
We Tommies in our trenches die.
And all in the name of freedom, sir,
Though few of us understand why.
Yet officers like you abound, sir.
Fornicating and sciving at the rear.
Forever wine, women and song, sir
With only the clap to fear.
But your soft posting is an illusion, sir.
In the end the war always wins.
Notice the Cross-Bones of Death, sir,
And the skull above it that grins.

Douglas John Hollands
The Duke of Wellington's Regiment

A SQUADDIE'S LAMENT

I'm lying here, drunk, in a corner
My head beating just like a drum.
I spent all last night in a boozer
And ended up flat on my bum.

My mates, they all lie in the gutter
Wondering just where they are.
Oh Lord, at last I remember.
We're in Tokyo - on R & R!!

Alan Guy
Royal Army Medical Corps

HELL

Across the great wide oceans
Korea is the spot
Where we're doomed to spend our time
In the land that God forgot.

Up with the snakes and lizards
Up where a man feels blue
Up in the middle of nowhere
A million miles from you.

We sweat, we freeze, we shiver
It's more than a man can stand
We're not supposed to be convicts
Just defenders of our land.

We're soldiers of the 1st Com. Div.
Earning a measly pay
Guarding people with millions
For four and six a day.

Nobody knows we are living
Nobody gives a damn
At home we are forgotten
We belong to Uncle Sam.

When we get to heaven
To Saint Peter we will tell
We're soldiers from Korea
And we've already lived in Hell!

Anon

"MOVING ON"

Sung with countless variations "Moving On" was to the English speaking troops in Korea as "Mademoiselle from Armentieres" was to the soldiers of the First World War.

> Chinkies coming up three-five-five
> The Yanks are pulling out in overdrive
> We're moving on, yes, we'll soon be gone,
> When you get to Kaesong, don't be too long,
> 'Cos we're moving on.
>
> The US Marine Corps are the best
> At always stopping for a rest
> We're moving on, yes, we'll soon be gone,
> When you get to Uijongbu, no time for a brew,
> 'Cos we're moving on.
>
> Here comes Poppa-san down the track
> With a twenty-five pounder on his back
> We're moving on, yes, we'll soon be gone,
> When you get to Inchon, don't be too long,
> 'Cos we're moving on.
>
> Hear the pitter patter of tiny feet
> It's the 1st Com Div. in full retreat
> We're moving on, yes, we'll soon be gone,
> When you get to Suwon, don't be too long,
> 'Cos we're moving on.
>
> The 'Die-hards' are attacking Plum Pudding Hill
> You'd better all have made a will
> We're moving on, yes, we'll soon be gone,
> When you get to Taejon, don't be too long,
> 'Cos we're moving on.
>
> See the Gooks coming over the ridge
> Heading like hell for Pintail bridge
> We're moving on, yes, we'll soon be gone,
> When you get to Kimchon, don't be too long,
> 'Cos we're moving on.

Here comes Momma-san down the track
With a blue-eyed baby riding on her back
We're moving on, yes, we'll soon be gone,
When you get to Taegu, no time for a brew,
   'Cos we're moving on.

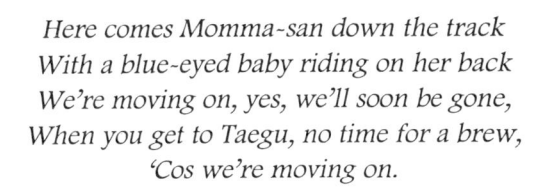

Ashes to ashes and dust to dust
If the Chinkies don't get you, then the Asahi must
We're moving on, yes, we'll soon be gone,
When you get to Pusan, don't cause a jam,
   'Cos we're moving on.

Anon

THE GENERAL'S TOOL

We Squaddies are paid but a pittance,
And we're never required to think,
Especially up at the sharp-end
Up there it's obedience or sink.
But it's a pretty safe bet (with the idiots we get)
That orders up front will be suicidal
Yet still we must obey, without any say,
Or be charged with being plain bloody idle.
Oh Tommy, you're only a laggard!
Oh Tommy, you're such a poor young fool.
Don't ever think for yourself, my lad.
You're nowt but a General's tool.

We Squaddies have fought in the jungles
Against guerrillas and swamps and all.
We've also fought in the mountains,
From the Alps to the heights of Nepal.
In deserts we've always been victorious,
With Kitchener and old Monty supreme,
And we fought the mad Mahdi without question
Though when we saw 'em we didn't half scream!
Oh Tommy, you're only a laggard!
Oh Tommy, you're such a poor young fool.
Don't ever think for yourself, my lad.
You're nowt but a General's tool.

We Squaddies have also known invasions
And floated on the tide to mined beaches.
To say nothing of scaling steep cliffs,
When we've clung on to nowt like leeches.
But whatever the tricks we resort to
And however great the Press hullabaloo,
When we hold out a paw, we get a quid, no more,
And then march off to our next Waterloo.
Oh Tommy, you're only a laggard!
Oh Tommy, you're such a poor young fool.
Don't ever think for yourself, my lad.
You're nowt but a General's tool.

Douglas John Hollands
The Duke of Wellington's Regiment

CAPTIVITY

The following section comes from a handmade book of poems written by anonymous prisoners of war in Camp 3, North Korea, in 1952.

The book was 'looked after' and eventually smuggled out of the POW camp on repatriation by Derek Hall, Black Watch.

The first poem was written in 1997 by D. S. Anderson, a friend of Derek Hall, as a tribute to the survivors of Camp 3.

P.O.W. CAMP 3
KOREA 1952

Precious book in a boot leather cover
Its paper now yellowed by time
Made long ago in a foreign land
Hand stitched down the jacket's spine.

As I turned each page of the tiny book
I couldn't help but feel
An empathy with every name
That the tiny book revealed.

The soldiers' names recorded
Had fought in the Korean War
Called to serve their countries
Until they could fight no more.

How did they feel on that fateful day
When entrapped by the enemy's hand
Would they have noticed the beauty
Of that hostile, alien land.

Men of many nationalities
Thrown together by conflict of war
Dispossessed and broken
Their dreams of a distant shore.

Indomitable is the will to survive
As experienced by the men of Camp 3
The burning desire to live at all cost
Whatever their future may be.

And when at last on that glorious day
That damnable battle was o'er
What were the feelings of every man
Rejoicing the end of a war.

So many questions I could ask
The answers never to know
My gratitude and humility
I quietly bestow.

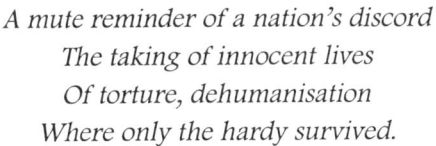

A mute reminder of a nation's discord
The taking of innocent lives
Of torture, dehumanisation
Where only the hardy survived.

The author of that tiny book
A survivor of Camp 3
Had fought for the right of freedom
So that mankind could live free.

D. S. Anderson
April 1997

THOUGHTS

I've walked the square for many a day.
What do I think of? What do I say?
I often think of a wasted life
About my family and my wife.

Of how I'm wasting precious years
Which won't return, in spite of tears.
I get no younger, day by day.
What do I think of? What do I say?

What should I say, I'm happy here?
Parted from those that I hold dear.
I sleep a while, and then I wake
And curse myself for my damned state.

The way we eat, the way we live,
All so really primitive.
To sum it up, my thoughts are these
To get back home and do what the hell I please.

Anon
POW Camp 3

PRISONER OF WAR

A long lost soul is what I am
Calling for help from my native land
Screaming in vain, not wanting to stay
A prisoner of war for another day.

Month upon month in this miserable place
Nothing forever will speed up the pace
Thinking of home each night and day
And knowing that we're prisoners yet another day.

Once we were men with a future bright,
Now we are ghosts, lost in the night.
Walking around with nothing to say
A prisoner of war for another day.

The questions asked by every guy
When to this hell will we bid goodbye?
Leaving Korea and its muddy decay,
A prisoner of war for another day.

The treatment is fair, the chow not bad,
If it wasn't for rice we would be glad,
But not very happy living this way
A prisoner of war for another day.

Everyone will be laughing with glee
On the day we are all set free.
No longer a prisoner having to say
A prisoner of war for another day.

Anon
POW Camp 3

A PHOTO

A photo is a treasure great
Especially in my present state.
To take it out, then put away.
I do this almost every day.

And as I look, I clearly see
All I desire back home for me.
A photo is a link between
The present time and what has been.

I do not envy, do not care
What others have, I have my share.
I only hope the one I see
Will turn from a photo to reality.

THE ANSWER

I know you are curious about my life in that strange land
As a prisoner of war in Korea, but how could you understand?
Many days and nights of misery, each hour filled with dread.
Not many of us left to speak for there's so many dead.

You ask about the treatment, was it good or bad?
I answer it is over now and I am very glad.
You ask about my captors, did I learn their habits or their traits?
I answer, I learned one thing, and that is how to hate.

You ask how I was captured and if I was wounded too.
Yes, I was wounded, but what does it mean to you?
I realise your idle interest, curiosity and wonder too
But even if I tried I couldn't explain this to you.

Of sickness, of death all about me, cold both night and day
That's the life of a prisoner and there's nothing more to say.
I hope this answers your questions and please forget you know I was a POW
Because I want to forget it too.

Anon
POW Camp 3

WHEN I RETURN

If, when I return to you
Free from this strange land
You find that I have changed, sweetheart
I hope you will understand.

Many months of loneliness
A life I can't describe,
I know has made some changes
That I can never hide.

I hope, my darling,
The changes that you see,
I hope they are constructive
And make a better me.

For I have learned the value
Of a buddy and a friend
And just how much, my darling,
We all in God depend.

I have seen men suffer
And never know relief
All because they wouldn't turn
Against their own belief.

And I have seen the opposite,
And this I can't forget.
A man that turned traitor
For just one cigarette.

All this, my darling,
Every word is true.
I only hope I can forget
When I return to you

Anon
POW Camp 3

THE INFANTRYMAN

The infantryman with a rifle on his shoulder and his flat feet on the ground
A canteen full of water and a pack weighing sixty pound.
With a hand grenade on his belt, a steel helmet on his head,
His entrenching tool is handy to make a foxhole for his bed.

When the weather is the foulest and the mud is ankle deep
You'll see him walking down the road on sore and blistered feet.
Just spitting and cursing at everything around
And calling all the officers as mud upon the ground.

The sergeants and corporals on a similar tryst
Just can't see why the officers enlist.
Where the bullets are the thickest and shells bursting all around
That's where you'll find the soldiers, lying on the ground.

But when the band is playing and the drums are sounding loud
In the ranks you'll see him marching and it's plain to see he's proud.
There's a medal on his chest which he displays with modest pride
In order to gain his award so many men have died.

Anon
POW Camp 3

TENDER LIPS

Think of me at night, when sleep is near
And I, who love you, am so far away.
Think of me then, and I will come to you
Ne'er leave you till the night turns back to day.

Stretch forth your hand through the depth of darkness
Another hand shall touch your fingertips.
And, as of old, my voice shall breathe your name
And press a kiss upon your tender lips.

HILLS OF KOREA

There's blood on the hills of Korea,
Tis the blood of the brave and the true
Of the nations that battle together
'Neath the banner of red, white and blue.

As men marched over the hills of Korea
To the hill where their enemy lay
They remembered the Brigadier's orders
That those hills must be taken today.

As they swung forward into action
Their faces unsmiling and stern
For they knew as they charged up that hillside
That many would never return.

Some thought of their wives and their mothers
Some thought of their sweetheart so fair
But all as they plodded and stumbled
Were softly whispering a prayer.

Now there's blood on the hills of Korea
It's the gift for the freedom they loved
May their names rest in glory forever
And their souls high in heaven above.

Anon
POW Camp 3

REMINISCENCE

OUR PALS

Tangok Military Cemetery, Pusan

You're not the first men to die for your country,
Nor the first men to lie in massed graves
By the shores of a far distant coastline
Where the Sea of Japan rolls its waves.

The flags of your countries they fly in the sun
That shone through the days of your brief.
Your friends will remember your joy and your fun
And your mothers will suffer their grief.

The goodbyes that we say as we drift through the night
Are happy and sad all at once;
For we don't know the day and we don't know the hour
When we, too, will be called to be judged.

The rest of us now will return to our homes
Through oceans and seas and canals,
To the lives that we left and the lovers we've missed;
But we'll never forget you - our pals.

Bill

We've just stopped here to say goodbye,
We're on our way back home;
We wish that you were coming too,
At least you're not alone.
Your cross is one of many, Bill,
In rows so neat and straight;
Your loss is one of many, too,
Goodbye, - Our dear old mate.

John T. Boyd
Royal Signals, King Troop, 28 Brigade

BLEAK DAY

The Battalion is going home
... before quitting Korea's shore
has one task more.

Sunday 14th September 1952
United Nations Cemetery, Pusan,
the Battalion parades 800 men
pay homage to their mates ...

At the sharp end no time to grieve
... now, so much emotion to compress
into last brief adieu.

... 800 choked infantrymen
raise barely a whimper
for hymns that are sung.

... The Last Post, eyes prickle, tears fall.
The silence that seems eternal
as videos run through the mind.
Reveille that nullifies reverie.

A walk through the field of crosses
painted pristine white,
in precise regimented rows
perfectly dressed to the right,
permanently on parade.

Here lie Eric, Gordon, Jamie,
side by side as when they fell
all is sanitized to make it look nice ...

... The image in my mind is ugly
each cross a blasted broken bloody body
... not laid neatly
lying scattered and in piles.

... A field of blood
reflected in the lowering brooding sky
is the image that fills my eyes
... anger in my heart
... guilt that I come home.

Peter Fisher
The King's Shropshire Light Infantry

AT REST

Beneath this foreign soil I lie,
And I think back to that time,
When under a bleak, cold alien sky
My life stopped in its prime.

I feel again, shock of the shell
That hit me on that day,
They gathered round me where I fell
I heard my comrades say.

'Hang on lad, don't go yet,
You're going home' they cried,
But I saw that their cheeks were wet,
And my heart knew that they lied.

They brought me to this place to lay,
Last Post, the bugles played,
I heard the rifles volley,
In this raw earth I was laid.

Here, I do not lie alone,
Rank after serried rank we lie,
Each one headed by a stone,
Why was it us, who had to die?

Since then the seasons have unwound,
And rain has soaked the soil,
And then the frost makes solid ground
Until the sun begins its toil.

Today an old friend made a call,
On his face, time shows its mark,
On my grave, his tears fall,
His thoughts are sad and dark.

Don't grieve old friend, for I'm not gone,
While in your thoughts I lie,
Your journey here was not forlorn,
Your tears you can dry.

In time, I know we'll meet again,
Don't worry my old friend,
And then we'll all forget the pain,
And sadness will have its end.

Anon

ODE TO A DEAD COCKNEY

He won't be comin' 'ome now, my Alfie, back to me;
He lies by another "tober" out there across the sea;
Born in the Old Kent Road 'e was, 'e knew the city's strife
But afore 'e died 'e wrote to me of the country's 'andsome life.

"Cor Mum the birds 'ere - they aint arf a mystery,
All of different colours - an' the bloomin' scenery.
They got sparrers 'ere of yella, an' blue an' green an' all,
They aint arf a pretty picture as they fly an' zoom an' stall.

But I wouldn't swap it Muvver for the Smoke wiv its dirty grates,
An' old Nelson standin' up there wiv the pigeons round 'is plates,
An' 'is one mince pie a starin' across the roofs each day
You can almost 'ear 'im shouting - come on boy! this way;
But I won't keep 'im waiting long Ma, it can't take much time now,
Afore I'm back there wiv yer in the bar at the Old Dun Cow.

An' then they sent 'im up the front, one night when the moon was bright.
'e dodged the bullets an' the shells - I bet 'e got a fright!
An' then they come an' told me 'e died like a soldier should
Fightin' for someone else's rights - just like I knew 'e would.

So 'e won't be comin' 'ome no more, my Alfie, back to me,
'e's underneath the rory wiv eyes that cannot see.
Or is 'e in the Smoke now? Sittin' up on Nelson's stand?
I like to think it's so, mate - so's I know 'e's near at 'and.

Mike Mogridge
Royal Fusiliers (The City of London Regiment)

THE FORGOTTEN WAR

Somewhere out there in a valley
In a country so far away
Is the grave of a British soldier
Who had never intended to stay.

He went there to fight an aggressor
And died in a wall of flame
Everyone knows where he came from
But nobody knows his name.

He lies all alone in silence
In the blood soaked soil of the land
And the reason why he lies there
No one will understand.

The name of this place is Korea
Where so many brave men gave their lives
But nobody seems to remember
Only parents, sweethearts and wives.

Nobody won in this conflict
It is still north and south as before
What a total waste of human life
This cruel and stupid war.

So let's stop and think for a moment
And all start to wonder and then
Reflect on how this could happen
And not let it happen again.

S. G. Buss
The Royal Leicestershire Regiment

I REMEMBER

Where were you when they
"Let loose the dogs of war"?
Were you a seasoned warrior
Or just a boy?
But, never mind and show no fear
We will send you to Korea.
Do you remember the tales your
Grandfather told?
Of mud and dust, the heat and the cold
And living like rats
In holes in the ground.
Do you remember "Standing your Ground"?
Shaking with fright while the
Shells fell around
And the bullets and guns made
That "GOD" fearing sound.
I still remember, that first bayonet charge
Running and screaming, afraid to be hurt,
Just to gain a few yards of war ravaged dirt.
Can you still hear the screams
As your friends fell beside you?
And you stood as a man
With your courage inside you.
Politicians spoke, with smug satisfaction,
"This is only a police action".
We fought tooth and nail
From our holes in the ground
And always remember those sights
And the sounds
Another night and a day "GOD" did give
But, many had died but, many more lived.
I remember my grandfather
And his stories of war,
Of Mons and Flanders
From "The war to end war".
Just blood and guts
Korea - a fancy "Police Action"?
THIS, WAS BLOODY WAR

Ron Leader
The Black Watch

FOR THOSE WHO WERE "THERE"

Who remembers the "forgotten war"?
Does anyone still care?
'Bout the battle at Imjin River?
Why not ask those who were there?

Ask them of death and dying
As the sound of battle filled the air.
Ask them if they remember,
Ask those men, those who were there!

The Infantry at "Middlesex Hill"
They fought, they did their share.
They won't forget the battle.
They can't, 'cause they were there!

Through the searing heat of summer,
In winter, cold beyond compare,
They faced an enemy ever ruthless,
Oh yes, they know that they were there!

There were thoughts of capture, torture,
And other fears they had to bear,
Still they fought the cause of freedom,
At freedom's calling, they were there!

In the land of morning calm,
Men of land, and sea, and air,
Army, Navy, and the Air Force,
Side by side, all were there!

And in this place so far away,
Was born comradeship so rare,
Where men who fought together
Still remember they were there.

The "forgotten war", Korea,
Now their memories they all share,
If you want to know what happened,
Go on, just ask those who were there!

Brian L. Porter

THE SIXTEEN HUNDRED

This poem is dedicated to all prisoners who died in Camp 5, North Korea, the majority were Americans, many of them very young.

Not a bugle was heard, not a funeral beat
Not even a drum sounding the retreat
As over the ice the corpses were hurried
To the hill where those GIs are buried
Six feet, by two feet, by one foot deep
In a Korean hill they sleep
Young and old all wondering why
The sixteen hundred had to die
No little white cross with their name
But they are not buried in shame
Although they lie in unknown graves
Sixteen hundred American braves
No useless caskets enclose their breasts
GI clothing for their last rest
All colours of men, brown, black and white
Sixteen hundred faded lights
A pill, a powder, medicine of any kind
Or should we say a stronger mind
Could have saved them from yonder hill
Sixteen hundred laying still
In their illness tossing and turning
Most of then knew there would be no returning
Some went easy some with pain
Sixteen hundred died in vain
When we go home to enjoy our fill
They are still there on that lonely hill
Forgotten by some
Remembered by most
Sixteen hundred in their Last Post

Jack Arnall
Royal Artillery

BEFORE ENDEAVOURS FADE

Dedicated to all those who paid the supreme sacrifice in defence of the principles of freedom.

> Let not their glory vanish
> With the setting of the sun.
> Let every generation
> See their justice done.
>
> They testify in silence
> From each known, and unknown grave;
> They did not live to witness
> The world they fought to save!
>
> Honour still their memory,
> And each hasty promise made,
> That they might be remembered,
> Before endeavours fade!

Denis J. Woods
45 Field & 20 Field Royal Artillery

NOT FORGOTTEN

To commemorate my visit to Korea in April 1996 and the final resting place of the fallen in Pusan.

> Standing still, in prayer to meet
> All those resting at my feet.
> So many in the sacred ground
> Silence greets me, all around.
> Dear God, this question I create
> "When will love replace the hate?".
> It seems, that when a comrade falls
> Everyone his name recalls.
> T'is better still, in place of strife
> That we recall his name in life.
> So many crosses, so many graves.
> The price that power-mad mankind craves.
> Show us dear God another way
> So we can live tomorrow, and another day.

T. J. Adkins
The Royal Fusiliers (City of London Regiment)

THE PHANTOM PIPER

It is silent now out in the valley,
Save the wind in the rusting barbed wire -
And the trenches have crumbled to nothing,
And the jeep tracks all covered in mire.
The paddy is barren and wasted;
The creek is reduced to a brook -
For it's forty long years
Since the pain and the tears -
When they fought for a hill called 'The Hook'.

When the shooting and killing were over,
And the armistice came into force;
They left their positions to nature,
And withdrew - they had little recourse.
Then they placed a large strip as a buffer,
Between both the south and the north,
And they banned the Koreans' admittance,
So the fighting would cease from thenceforth.

The valley's now peopled with spirits,
So the troops who keep guard often say;
And sometimes they hear voices calling
At night time as well as by day.
And at dusk when the daylight is fading,
And the hill tops are each bathed in red
A phantom's heard piping a pibroch -
Lamenting the glorious dead.

(from "Once Upon a Hill Top")

W. A. (Tony) Thorn
The King's Regiment (Liverpool)

REMEMBRANCE DAY REFLECTIONS

I heard a distant bugle call on a Hampshire hill today,
and my thoughts turned to another hill, on a very different day.
A day that I remember well, when buglers played Last Post,
and faces of men who gave their all return to me like ghosts.
Footsloggers, tankies, engineers, gunners and supporting arms.
From cities, villages, country towns, from the factories and farms
came young men from all walks of life, to man the Imjin line.
That lilting bugle cries out still for those good mates of mine.

I heard once more that bugle call on a Hampshire hill today.
And I remembered other hills as the last note trailed away.
That bugler played for Gloucester lads who fought so gallantly
'til bullets, water, food were gone, at a place called Solma-ri.
Chinese bugles had onwards urged ten thousand across Imjin's waters
against six hundred Gloucester boys, supported by C Troop's mortars.
Comradeship, pride, esprit-de-corps helped those lads survive,
and a Gloucester bugle defiantly played, at the end, on Hill 235.

I thought I heard the bagpipes skirl on a Hampshire hill today,
and I recalled another hill, and a very different day.
A hill in North Korea where a piper played his tune
to stir the young Jocks onward under a bright November moon.
No tree, no bush, no blade of grass went undisturbed that day
by mortar, shell, machine-gun fire, as I heard that piper play.
I watched the Chinese remove by night their dead, others barely alive
from that other place, that other hill that we knew as '355'.

I heard again that piper's tune on a Hampshire hill today,
and I know it was not the wind, no wind that tune could play.
I closed my eyes and I could see Jocks, heroes every man,
and I saw once more the dark caubeen of an Ulster Rifleman.
Fusiliers from Northumberland, light infantry from Shropshire,
field gunners, mortarmen, long-range snipers, drop-shorts.
Too many died, like falling leaves that the winds have blown away,
but I remember them all as the bugles sound on each Remembrance Day.

That bugle call died in the wind on my Hampshire hill today.
Did I really hear those notes? Did I hear that piper play?
Was it just imagination? Was it just the breeze?
Did I really fight that war in the land across the seas?
The bugles shrill, Last Post for today, Reveille for tomorrow.
The Forest's Flowers, the pipes lament, to heads held high in sorrow.
To me those notes ring out today for good mates across the sea
who lie forever in a foreign land, that Korea would be free.

On my Hampshire hill those notes resound, not only for 'My War'.
Other bugle calls ring out over hill, and field, and moor.
Other pipers play laments at our Cenotaphs and Halls,
Those pipes and bugles sound today for the dead of all our wars.
Today's youth may not comprehend why we need our special day,
But today's youth has never heard my ghostly piper play
on that hill in North Korea, nor heard the Chinese bugles bray.
And we should pray that they never will, at the Cenotaph, today.

Jim Jacobs
170 Independent Mortar Battery, Royal Artillery

KOREA

They went as boys came back as men they served their countries well
For they had seen the worst life for them it seemed like hell
They fought against increasing odds the weather and the foe
They were taken to the edge where few men want to go.
They did it right they did it well for all the world to see
For freedom was their only aim not conquest, prize or fee
Their shattered limbs and broken bodies on the battlefield
Left us with scars so deep inside that they will never heal
The sound of battle the cries of men are sounds we cannot shed
Those sounds are tattooed on our minds its always in our heads
For we have seen the worst of life in every shape and form
The longest hour, the darkest hour,
is the one before the dawn.

Roy (Brummy) Reece
Royal Army Medical Corps. 26 Field Ambulance (No1 CCP)

THE FIELD OF CROSSES

In memory of my comrades who lie in the United Nations Cemetery, Pusan, and those whose graves are now lost forever, somewhere in Korea. The original graves in Pusan were marked with wooden crosses. They were later replaced with bronze plaques.

The years have passed in plenty
Since the time that I was there,
Along with countless others,
Their burden I would share.

But whereas I came home again,
Perhaps not quite the same
As when I left these shores to fight,
In the land with the funny name!

I often think of those who stayed,
Detained against their will,
Beneath a field of wooden crosses,
On the side of a sun-baked hill.

What price the golden glory
In the winning of the fight,
With you not here to share it,
But gone forever from our sight.

But you are not forgotten,
And this I remember too.
But for the grace of God above,
I'd have shared that field with you!

Denis J. Woods
45 Field Regiment
and 20 Field Regiment Royal Artillery

UNITED THEY STOOD

They came from the lands of the Leek and the Thistle,
The Maple, the Kiwi and Kangaroo,
To join comrades-in-arms and fight off oppression,
In a land far away of which nobody knew.

In fierce bitter winters and strong summer sun
They fought with such fury that the battles were won.
Now a peace, although fragile, remains in that land,
Through the bravery of men and God's almighty hand.

THE KOREAN VETERAN

Long forgotten by their country,
Men who fought on distant land,
Some who died in mortal combat,
Slaughtered by a foreign hand.
Young men wounded, young men crying,
Young men bleeding, young men dying.
Was their sacrifice in vain?
Was their effort worth the pain?

Happy children, so beguiling -
Laughing, jumping, skipping, smiling,
Fill the land of Morning Calm -
All now safe and free from harm.
Thanks to every mother's son
Who fought for each and every one;
Showing that despite the pain,
Their valiant efforts weren't in vain!

Alan Guy
Royal Army Medical Corps

ABSENT VETERANS

Would that you could wander still
Through grassy fields by wooded hill
When morning birdsong fills the air
And yet another spring is here.

If only you could still feel sun
Upon your face when winter's done
And smell sweet-scented flowers fair
When yet another summer's here.

But fate decided otherwise
And you, beneath Korean skies
A gallant band of heroes lie
Your duty done, your merit high.

No changing seasons can erase
That one familiar name, that face
That comes and lingers with each thought
Of those with whom we lived and fought.

THE MEMORIAL BENCH

Written for dedication of a bench along the river at Bedford.

This bench by riverside is blest by thoughts
That reach beyond these shores to distant parts
An eastern land, Korea, where countless hills
Look down on paddy-fields, and white cranes fly
Where quietly flows the Imjin now and there's
But scarce a sign of that forgotten war
Which we, much younger, knew for we were there.
And having fought, some safely home returned
To tell of those who stayed, in battle killed.
So if you seat yourself to pause a while
Upon this wooden bench, to contemplate
And watch the swiftly running Ouse, the swans,
The ducks that sail contentedly along
Within the shade of trees bespeckled by the sun,
Then please, with kindly prayer remember those
Who, if they had not paid the price they did,
Could now be watching this fair scene like you.

David U. R. Lidstone
The Gloucestershire Regiment

BRITISH SOLDIER

Just one more British soldier in a poet's 'foreign field',
Just one more 'silent corner' with its 'richer dust' concealed,
Just one more mother's sadness, and a young girl's heavy heart,
Just one more act of madness, the war that had to start.

Just one more life, unlived and wasted,
No chance to judge its joys untasted,
No time now for growing older,
For just one more British Soldier.

WARS WILL NEVER END

"A war to end all wars" they said.
Slowly we counted up our dead
And mothers came to learn to live
Without their sons they'd had to give.

Wives and sweethearts also found
The pain that "Greater love" had bound
Them all to wasteful sacrifice
For soon it was to happen twice
In people's lives and even more
The losses grew in yet another war.

Old adversaries marched again
Young men fell and suffered pain
The Jew faith was burned away
Flesh and bone became decay
Cities flamed and buildings crumbled
Across the world the cannons rumbled
And though that war did one day end
No one learnt, hearts did not mend.

Korea, Falklands, The Gulf and others
Brothers even fought their brothers
Nature's Law no comfort gives
Eternally, while Mankind lives
The fittest always will survive
Until there's no one left alive.

George E. Loudoun
27 Brigade Signals Troop

THE SUNDAY PARADE

On the occasion of dedication of new colours to the Hertfordshire Branch BKVA, 20th September 1992.

On parade they formed in ranks of fours
As forebears had done in bygone years
Led, by band and banner in the afternoon
Stepping off to a marching tune.
Each man in time, with head held proud
And swing of arms along the road
And all, in those serried ranks of four
Remembered that forgotten war
In that land, ten thousand miles away,
Korea, as if just yesterday.
Of foxholes dug in frozen earth,
The cloying stench of fear and death,
The icy winds, the blinding snow
Before light of dawn, "All men stand to"
And then "Stand down, stand at ease"
Let's brew up, before we freeze.
Fleeting mem'ries flash through one's mind
As down gently sloping hill we wind.
Into the Abbey, standing there
With our heads abowed in prayer.
We think about those years long gone
And mates who didn't make it home
Then comes the colours' dedication
Performed before the congregation.
"Form ranks", and we march back again.
Lovely day, it didn't rain.
We were provided with a tasty snack
By our hosts, when we got back.
We look around and greet old friends,
Smiling faces, shaking hands.
Off we go our separate ways,
"See you again, there'll be other days".
In the meantime, until then,
"In the morning, we will remember them".

Bob Guess
Royal Norfolks

KOREAN VETERANS

Age now the enemy
Korean veterans one and all,
Age and illness we must stall
Youth just amounts to memory.

We visualise faces, bygone days
Lads fighting fit in many ways,
Changed to men in very quick time
Loss of pals along the line.

Members making their last stand
Fading memories of a distant land,
Now it's weariness and age
Must keep going at every stage.

Happy smiles good times stay
In one's mind always lay,
Forgotten darkness of the night
With Morning Calm the dawning light.

Cold days then, paid a shilling
Pension now just as chilling,
Known as the forgotten war
Shoot outs, but no final score.

Meet with your Veterans' Branch
Make the effort at every chance,
Enjoy the company of yesteryear
Just a chat and one more beer.

Fred A. Almey
RAF 1903 AOP Flight

A CHANGE OF HEART

For forty years and more
After National Service and bloody war
My medals I never wore
Consigned them to a drawer.

But with procession of the years
Memories poignant fraught with tears,
Just once I had to go
My medals for to show.

Remembrance Sunday nineteen ninety-five
Giving thanks that I was alive,
For Eric heart-broken sorrow
He never saw the morrow
- did not come home.

Medals bright and gay
Worn with pride and honour that day
"Worn once only Eric, just for thee;
Received not your medals of the-line
You shall have mine
Buried 'neath your remembrance tree".

A milestone in my life achieved
Fresh prospects and vistas to foresee,
Seek and join the Veterans of Korean War
Opens up another door;
'I have come home' they are all as me
Never to forget comrades whom they grieved
- I am not alone, I am their clone.

I belong again to that brotherhood of the line
The comradeship that was yours and mine
- and then I see that I was blind
That medals are a symbol of the mind
- like Flander's poppies.

Medals displayed do fulfil a role
Together with Standard dipped,
Honouring a fellow veteran
Who in his sleep, his life away has slipped.

His wife, daughters and friends
Proud that we were 'on parade'
Sharing their grief and sorrow
His comrades to the very end.

It is not showing off -
It is in remembrance of that elite few
Who stood together in strife,
To those who came through,
Survived - to those who lost their life.

Forgive me Eric that I change my mind
My medals shall be yours in time
But for today let me wear them and find
Renewal of that comradeship sublime.

Peter Fisher
The King's Shropshire Light Infantry

COUNSELLING

(From Once Upon a Hill Top)

It was May and the time of reunion,
With the lads from the 'Pool' and beyond
So we met as before in the Drill Hall,
Each linked by the same common bond.

As I sat and I supped and I chatted,
I noticed the lad on my right.
His face was all smiles and good humour;
He was mellow, but nowhere near tight.

"Good evening", says he with a twinkle,
A glass full of beer in his hand.
"I come to these 'do's' fairly often,
But there's one thing I don't understand".

"We fought for our Queen and our country;
We sweated and blinded and cursed.
We dug and we marched and we laboured;
And climbed all them hills fit to burst.

The Colonel was back in his hoochie;
The transport behind in the rear;
While we were up front at the sharp end,
Full of nervous exhaustion and fear.

Each night we 'stood to' in the evening -
And again with the coming of dawn;
And we went on patrol in the valley,
Making sure we were back with the morn.

At times it was downright alarming,
Especially at night in the dark;
And when them Chinese blew their bugles,
I tell you it wasn't no lark!

You knew when them devils was coming -
They let fly with all that they had;
And them shells and them bullets and mortars
Were at times so intense we went mad.

Yet we stood and we watched and we waited,
Until the bombardment should stop.
For that was the moment we dreaded -
When those Chinkies came 'over the top'!

You forgot in the heat of the battle
All the things you were told at the start;
Like when to fire 'single' or 'rapid' -
Or stick your cold steel through his heart.

Once battle is joined it's sheer bedlam -
All bodies and bangers and blood;
And trenches all broken and battered;
And squaddies all covered in mud.

The enemy charge in their hundreds -
In hundreds they lie down and die;
Forever they seem to keep coming,
Never mind how your bullets may fly.

By now they are close to and screaming -
The ones who aren't wounded or dead;
And you struggle with butt and with bayonet,
And thrust at his stomach and head.

So busy you don't seem to notice
That the tide is at last on the turn;
And the groups that are still joined in battle,
Get the order that bids them return.

Then suddenly everything's quiet;
Except for the moaning and cries;
And you look for your mates mid the cordite;
And glance where your officer lies.

He's smiling beneath his steel helmet,
But his face is as white as the snow;
And the blood has congealed on his tunic,
Just where his medals should go.

So you cover his face with a blanket;
And you gather the lads for a chat.
Then you count up the dead and the living;
And those that can walk, you lead back.

And that was the end of the battle;
At least for the night that was passed.
Though little we felt or applauded;
For we knew it would not be the last.

Now we meet every year in the Drill Hall;
And we drink and we talk with our mates;
And it's this that we need more than 'counsel';
Whatever the manual states.

All I need is a pint and a comrade;
You can 'stuff' all your trouble and strife.
'Counselling'? You can forget it,
I already get that from my wife!"

W. A. (Tony) Thorn
The King's Regiment (Liverpool)

IN REMEMBRANCE

On 11th March 1987 Her Majesty the Queen unveiled a memorial in St. Paul's Cathedral to all those who gave their lives in the Korean War.

Spring on the steps of St. Paul's,
And the wind blowing cold from the river,
Half a lifetime on.
Like birds they come,
Gathering in regimental rows,
And though their plumage
May be fading with the years,
Their hearts are strong, their loyalties secure.
No order given, yet suddenly with one accord,
They turn, and falling into silence,
Enter, with reverence and pride,
The great dome behind.
They sit awhile in thought,
Then, rising for their Queen,
They sing again the old familiar hymns,
And offer up their prayers, to glorify the dead.
A piper plays a lone lament,
While in the crypt below,
Her Majesty unveils the stone
That will recall for evermore,
The dead of the Korean War,
Whose graves now lie in faraway Pusan.
Then bugle calls,
As once before on Gloucester Hill,
Echoing in the vast void above;
Primeval, haunting notes,
That circle ever upwards,
Round and round,
Like the souls of dead friends,
Seeking eternal rest.
'Faith of our fathers', the final hymn,
And then, as Queen and State depart,
A moment to reflect, and say farewell
To those who, in the springtime of their youth,
Gave us their lives, that we might live in truth.

W. A. (Tony) Thorn
The King's Regiment (Liverpool)

WHERE ARE YOU NOW?

Dedicated to all my comrades who fought in the Korean War of 1950-53 especially those who now lie in the United Nations Cemetery in Pusan, and other places (detained against their will).

>Where are you now, my comrades of yesteryear
>Who shared 'the great adventure' with me
>In our youth, once held so very dear,
>When brave, we spurned all waking thoughts of fear?
>
>Some, I know, still rest in that far place
>That is now their own, and sleep their sleep
>'Neath plaques of bronze, to indicate the grave
>Wherein they lie, in consecrated grace!
>
>And those who stand above you on the sward,
>Be they loved ones, friends, or merely passers-by,
>Should pay their homage, deep, your just reward,
>For once you held the sword of Freedom high!
>
>In regimented lines your markers stand,
>You who were once young and vibrant men,
>Soldiers in a far off, foreign land,
>Who bravely fought, and made your final stand!
>
>And those of you who rest, we know not where,
>Who pays homage to your departed souls?
>Your loved ones? Yes; for they will ever care,
>And on Remembrance Sunday say their prayer!
>
>And you, my comrades, you who yet still are!
>But shadows of what mighty men we were.
>Do you still follow a happy, healthy star,
>Or are you, like me, only robust from afar?
>
>Do you recall, when young and in our prime,
>And danger made the blood race through our veins?
>Do moments, fixed in time, stay in your mind,
>Like images of a three dimensional kind?

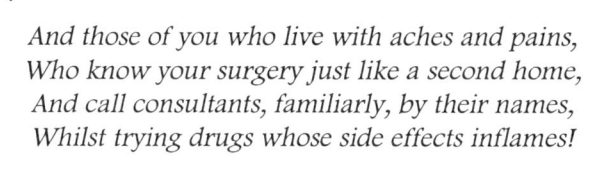

And those of you who live with aches and pains,
Who know your surgery just like a second home,
And call consultants, familiarly, by their names,
Whilst trying drugs whose side effects inflames!

Are your dreams, like mine, the cause of sweat
That soak your pillow, after dreaming in your bed?
The images, so real even yet
Ensuring that we who live will not forget!

And do you still attend re-union 'Do's',
To reminisce what happened, when, and where?
Getting dates and places mixed up through the booze,
About a war that rarely made the news!

Do you ever see your listener's glazing eyes
Avert from you, embarrassed, or in shame?
And turn their faces from you to the skies,
Because they think that you are telling lies!

I go no more to meetings of that kind,
Preferring to recall us as we were,
When we were very young, and in our prime,
Before we each succumbed to passing time!

Where are you now, you who once were brave?
Who fought your inner fears, as warriors do,
Do you ever wonder why we fought to save
That far off land that is our comrades' grave?

And do you sit, like me, in darkening light,
And think of those whose bodies now are dust?
Or do you think such memories should take flight,
And banished, yes forever, from our sight?

I do not know the answer to these thoughts
Nor do I think I ever really will.
Was Freedom worth the price our comrades bought?
If not - why was that bitter conflict ever fought ...?

Denis J. Woods
45 Field Regiment and 20 Field Regiment, Royal Artillery

50th ANNIVERSARY

Don't worry boys we are coming
Though we are 12,000 miles away.
We are keeping a promise we made to you
Fifty years ago today
When we left you in a Pusan graveyard
And there you had to stay.

We may now be old and grey
But we are keeping our promise to come back some day.
Form up by the crosses that stand row on row.
Thank you for the sacrifice you made so long ago
When we fought side by side in the bleak winter snow.

This time a band will beat the retreat.
We'll bring wives and friends for you to meet.
When night time falls last post will be played
We'll salute the place upon where you are laid.

A new Standard to honour you we'll carry with pride
As tears we'll try so hard to hide.
Some of us you won't recognise
For on us time and pain have taken their toll.
But we set ourselves an achievable goal
To return no matter what the cost
To see again the pals we had lost.

You know once more we'll have to part
But you'll stay forever in our heart.
And as long as there is a Korean Vet alive
You can rest assured your memory will survive.

R. Miller
The Duke of Wellington's Regiment

The BRITISH KOREAN VETERANS ASSOCIATION

The BKVA was formed at an inaugural meeting held at Imphal Barracks, York, on Saturday 26th September 1981 through the amalgamation of The National Association of Korean War Veterans (UK) and The British Korean Veterans Association.

We are members of the International Federation of Korean War Veterans Associations, whose headquarters are in Seoul, South Korea, and which promotes the interests of all who fought in the Korean War.

The prime objective of the BKVA is to organise, develop, enter into and carry out or co-operate in any endeavour for the benefit of men and women of all ranks who served in the Korean War, June 1950 - July 1953, and subsequent Peacekeeping Forces, or for the benefit of their widows and dependents, and generally to promote their welfare and the relief of distress.

The BKVA is non-political and offers comradeship to all those who served in Korea. There are currently fifty-nine branches in Great Britain and one in Northern Ireland. New branches are formed as the need arises.

We maintain close links with other ex-service organisations of which many of our Veterans are also members.

The BKVA's authoritative body is the National Council, whose membership is made up of elected Executive Officers, elected National Council Officers and one member from each of the Association's ten areas. All are volunteers.

The Association's journal 'Morning Calm' is published twice a year. Many branches also publish their own newsletter or magazine.

Throughout the year, in many parts of the country events are organised which are open to all Korean Veterans. These occasions allow veterans, together with their families, to come together and renew their fellowship.

The Association holds an Annual General Meeting in October, which incorporates some social events. In addition many branches organise special functions to which they invite members of other branches.

In co-operation with the Korean Veterans' Association, Seoul, in the Republic of Korea, the BKVA organises an official re-visit programme, details of which are available from branch secretaries.

The BKVA maintains strong links with the Korean Embassy, Korean Residents Associations and Travel Organisations in the UK, where there is an interest joining together for cultural ties and joint projects.

We recognise and appreciate the willingness of Korean people in the UK to support our Veterans and their needs.

The present membership is about 4,500 and growing. Every effort is being made to recruit more members - we are aware that there are still many hundreds of Korean Veterans who would benefit from membership in the BKVA. We also encourage Associate Membership of individuals and organisations supportive of our objectives.

Membership details are available from

Brian Hough
11 Wardle Brook Walk, Hattersley, Hyde, Cheshire, SK14 3JG
Telephone 0161 368 4407

Further information about the Association is obtainable from the General Secretary

Frank Ellison, BEM, JP
12 Fields Crescent, Hollingworth, Hyde, Cheshire, SK14 8JR
Telephone 01457 763699
Fax 01457 766748

PATRONS

General Sir Anthony Farrar-Hockley, GBE, KCB, DSO, MC, M.Litt.
Major General Sir Peter Downward, KCVO, CB, DSO, DFC.
Keith M. Taylor, FCIM, FIMgt, FInstD.

NATIONAL OFFICERS

President	-	Major General A. C. Birtwistle CB, CBE, DL, MA
Chairman	-	Colonel George M. Gadd
Treasurer	-	Jim E. Wilkinson, SBStJ
Secretary	-	Frank Ellison, BEM, JP
Overseas Co-ordinator	-	Frank Fallows
National Projects Officer	-	George Lakey
Welfare Adviser	-	David St John Griffiths
Korean Liaison Officer	-	Alan Guy
Editor, The Morning Calm	-	Reuben Holroyd, BEM
PRO / Recruitment Officer	-	Brian Hough
Registrar	-	John Marsden
Supplies Officer	-	Peter Melville

TRUSTEES

Major General A. C. Birtwistle, CB, CBE, DL, MA
M. A. Geoghegan, JP
T. A. Moore
N. F. Townsend, DL, JP

BRITISH FORCES IN THE KOREAN WAR

Edited by Ashley
Cunningham-Boothe
and Peter Farrar

Price £15
including post
and packing

First published in 1988 by the British Korean Veterans Association

Available from

Frank Ellison, BEM, JP
12 Fields Crescent, Hollingworth, Hyde, Cheshire, SK14 8JR

Cheques payable to BKVA